ROUTLEDGE LIBRARY EDITIONS: PHONETICS AND PHONOLOGY

Volume 15

LARYNGEAL FEATURES AND LARYNGEAL NEUTRALIZATION

LARYNGEAL FEATURES AND LARYNGEAL NEUTRALIZATION

LINDA LOMBARDI

LONDON AND NEW YORK

First published in 1994 by Garland Publishing, Inc.

This edition first published in 2019
by Routledge
2 Park Square, Milton Park, Abingdon, Oxon OX14 4RN

and by Routledge
711 Third Avenue, New York, NY 10017

Routledge is an imprint of the Taylor & Francis Group, an informa business

© 1994 Linda Lombardi

All rights reserved. No part of this book may be reprinted or reproduced or utilised in any form or by any electronic, mechanical, or other means, now known or hereafter invented, including photocopying and recording, or in any information storage or retrieval system, without permission in writing from the publishers.

Trademark notice: Product or corporate names may be trademarks or registered trademarks, and are used only for identification and explanation without intent to infringe.

British Library Cataloguing in Publication Data
A catalogue record for this book is available from the British Library

ISBN: 978-1-138-60364-6 (Set)
ISBN: 978-0-429-43708-3 (Set) (ebk)
ISBN: 978-1-138-31788-8 (Volume 15) (hbk)
ISBN: 978-1-138-31794-9 (Volume 15) (pbk)
ISBN: 978-0-429-45492-9 (Volume 15) (ebk)

Publisher's Note
The publisher has gone to great lengths to ensure the quality of this reprint but points out that some imperfections in the original copies may be apparent.

Disclaimer
The publisher has made every effort to trace copyright holders and would welcome correspondence from those they have been unable to trace.

LARYNGEAL FEATURES AND LARYNGEAL NEUTRALIZATION

LINDA LOMBARDI

GARLAND PUBLISHING, INC.
NEW YORK & LONDON / 1994

Copyright © 1994 by Linda Lombardi
All rights reserved

Library of Congress Cataloging-in-Publication Data

Lombardi, Linda, 1961–
    Laryngeal features and laryngeal neutralization / Linda Lombardi.
      p.   cm. — (Outstanding dissertations in linguistics)
    Includes bibliographical references and index.
    ISBN 0–8153–1687–9
    1. Laryngeals (Phonetics) 2. Neutralization (Linguistics)
    3. Distinctive features (Linguistics)   I. Title. II. Series.
    P239.L66   1994
    414—dc20   93–33844
                                                                      CIP

Printed on acid-free, 250-year-life paper
Manufactured in the United States of America

CONTENTS

Preface	vii
Chapter 1. Laryngeal features of obstruents	1
1.1 Introduction	1
1.2 What laryngeal features are needed for phonology	15
Notes	21
Chapter 2. The feature [voice] and voicing assimilation	25
2.1 Introduction	25
2.2 Analyses	36
2.3 Predictions of possible theories	52
2.4 Other possible counterevidence	61
Notes	71
Chapter 3. Glottalization and aspiration	77
3.1 Overview of Laryngeal node neutralization	77
3.2 Constraint on the Laryngeal node	81
3.3 Constraint on single features	96
3.4 Constraint and Final Exceptionality	100
3.5 Spreading of aspiration	102
3.6 Apparent counterexamples to the theory	122
3.7 Summary	132
3.8 The Binding Hypothesis	135
Appendix	141
Notes	143

Chapter 4. Laryngeal phonology of sonorants   149

    4.1 Laryngeal features of sonorants   149
    4.2 Neutralization and sonorants   157
    4.3 Voice and sonorants at later levels   163

    Notes   173

Bibliography   175

Index   193

PREFACE

For their influence on this work, special thanks are due to John McCarthy, Ronald Boucher and Alison Taub. Other valuable influences in the course of my education came from Jane Grimshaw and from the rest of my dissertation committee: F. Roger Higgins, Alan Prince, and Lisa Selkirk. Various other sorts of support, for which I am also grateful, were provided by Kathy Adamczyk, Beth Jackendoff, and Molly Potter.

A revised version of parts of chapters 2 and 3 is, as of this writing, due to appear in *Natural Language and Linguistic Theory* entitled 'Laryngeal neutralization and syllable wellformedness.'

CHAPTER 1

LARYNGEAL FEATURES OF OBSTRUENTS

1.1 Introduction

The laryngeal features and laryngeal phonology have not been investigated in detail since the development of autosegmental phonology and feature geometry. Feature geometry provides the means to deal with some generalizations about laryngeal phonology that it was impossible to capture in previous systems. The most common phonological process involving laryngeal features is laryngeal neutralization, wherein all laryngeal distinctions are lost in syllable-final position. In a theory where segments consist of an unorganized set of feature specifications, there is no way to refer to the laryngeal features as a group that patterns together distinct from other possible groups of features. This makes it impossible to write the neutralization rule in a way that reflects its phonological naturalness.

In the framework of feature geometry, these groupings of features are part of the structure of a segment, expressed as dependency relations among features and abstract nodes dominating groups of features. It is thus possible to manipulate the laryngeal distinctions as a group, by manipulating the abstract Laryngeal Node that dominates the laryngeal features. This advance in phonological theory allows a vastly improved analysis of laryngeal neutralization as delinking of the Laryngeal node, as proposed by Clements (1985).

However, many questions remain as to the precise formulation of this rule. More detailed analysis, both of the phonology of individual languages and of the cross-linguistic phonological patterns involving neutralization, is required to answer this question. These issues are addressed in chapters 2 and 3. There I propose that neutralization is the result of a wellformedness condition that I call the Laryngeal Constraint: In languages that have laryngeal neutralization, a laryngeal node is only licensed in a particular syllabic configuration; elsewhere the node will delink to repair the violation of well-formedness. As I show in chapters 2 and 3, this approach to neutralization is required to correctly explain the typology of laryngeal neutralization.

Neutralization brings up questions about the segments that are unmarked in phonological rules and in the phoneme system of a language. Current theory has two ways of accounting for this kind of issue: underspecification and privative features. I will argue that in the case of laryngeal phonology these facts are accounted for by the hypothesis that the laryngeal features are privative. This is a necessary aspect of the delinking analysis of neutralization: it explains why neutralized obstruents are always voiceless unaspirated, and neutralized sonorants are always plain voiced (see chapters 3 and 4). If the features are privative, the negative values of these features are not present because they are nonexistent, and this explains both types of markedness facts. Underspecification theory predicts that [-voice] can be active in phonological derivations, and that [+voice] could sometimes be the output of neutralization. Since these predictions are both false, privative features rather than underspecification is the correct solution. The issue of the privativeness of the laryngeal features is addressed at many points throughout this study, as it is a central fact in laryngeal phonology. Privativeness of [voice] is discussed in in chapter 2, neutralization of multiple laryngeal contrasts in chapter 3, and the supporting evidence from sonorant neutralization in chapter 4. The remainder of chapter 1 will address the predictions of privative features with respect to patterns of laryngeal distinctions in phoneme systems.

Before the behavior of the laryngeal features in rules can be addressed, however, it is necessary to determine what the correct features are. Past work on laryngeal features has tended to be heavily influenced by questions of how these distinctions are produced physically. This has obscured the basic phonological issues that must be considered in postulating a feature system. This earlier attention to a very fine level of phonetic detail--much finer than is usually considered for, say, the place features--has obscured cross-linguistic generalizations and made these feature systems far more detailed than is correct for phonological purposes. The remainder of this chapter examines this issue, discussing why it is important to distinguish phonological from phonetic distinctions. I will argue that the correct feature system consists of three features, [voice], [glottalization] and [aspiration], which, as I have already mentioned, are single-valued.

The most influential past treatments of laryngeal features are those of Halle and Stevens (1971) and Lisker and Abramson (1964). Halle and Stevens propose four features: [stiff vocal cords], [slack v.c.], [spread glottis] and [constricted glottis]. Lisker and Abramson (1964) show that voiceless, voiced, and voiceless aspirated consonants can be distinguished by differences in Voice Onset Time. Although these are the standard references, phonologists rarely adopt either of these systems in phonological analyses. This suggests that these feature systems have not had much success in explaining phonological facts.

To begin I will discuss the problems with each of these theories, in sections 1.1.1 and 1.1.2. Section 1.1.3 will discuss the theory first proposed by Kingston (1985, 1990) that laryngeal distinctions are bound to the release of a consonant. Section 1.2 will then argue for a feature system consisting of three privative laryngeal features of voicing, aspiration and glottalization.

1.1.1 Halle and Stevens (1971)

The feature system of Halle and Stevens (1971) (H&S) for obstruents is given in (1), using the features [spread glottis], [constricted glottis], [stiff vocal cords], [slack vocal cords].

(1)

	1	2	3	4	5	6	7	8	9
	b_1	b	p	p_k	b^h	p^h	ɓ	?b	p?
[sg]	-	-	-	+	+	+	-	-	-
[cg]	-	-	-	-	-	-	+	+	+
[stiff]	-	-	+	-	-	+	-	-	+
[slack]	-	+	-	-	+	-	-	+	-

b_1: lax voiceless stop
p_k: lightly aspirated (Korean)
b?: voiced laryngealized
p?: ejective

In this system, aspiration is marked by [spread glottis] and glottalization by [constricted glottis]. Voicing is not marked by a single feature, but is determined by the combination of the values for the features [stiff] and [slack].

A number of objections to this system have been summarized by Keating (1988)[1]. The main problems have to do with the feature system's representation of voicing. The phonetic issue is simply that voiced sounds are not always made with the state of the vocal chords that H&S assume. H&S developed their system using mainly modeling of the vocal tract, rather than instrumental data of actual glottal configurations. Keating points out for instance that although stiffening of the vocal chords would indeed prevent voicing, this is not how people actually produce voiceless sounds. Usually a spreading gesture is used, but the H&S feature [spread] entails aspiration.

There are also phonological problems with the representation of voicing in the Halle and Stevens features. There is no simple description of voiced sounds: no one feature will group all voiced sounds as opposed to all voiceless sounds. H&S give no evidence that these are the features that are needed to write phonological rules. (The only uses I know of them is Hayes (1984)[2] and unpublished work by Levin (1984).) Finally, there are major problems with the systems of contrasts that can be represented with this system. The features allow phonological representation of laryngeal distinctions that are never used contrastively, such as implosive/voiced laryngealized, and yet they do not allow representation of all possible phonetic contrasts. In Section 1.2 I will discuss why this is an important theoretical issue, and what contrasts need to be accounted for.

The practice of phonologists has mostly been to simply use a feature [voice] rather than the H&S system. Writers also use the features [constricted glottis] and [spread glottis] to designate glottalized and aspirated consonants, without adopting the whole system. This is basically equivalent to having a feature system consisting of [voice], [asp] and [gl]. As I will show later, this intuition seems to be correct.

1.1.2 Lisker and Abramson (1964): Voice Onset Time

The other standard framework of laryngeal distinctions is that of Voice Onset Time, following the work of Lisker and Abramson (1964). This theory is based solely on phonetic data. As far as I know this framework has never been incorporated into phonological analysis except in the work of Goldstein and Browman (1986, also Browman and Goldstein 1986), discussed below. Nonetheless phonologists do seem to consider this one of the basic references on the subject of laryngeal distinctions, despite the fact that they make no attempt to integrate it into their own analyses. Because of this it is important to make it clear that the VOT framework, though it is a correct phonetic generalization, does not allow the construction of a usable phonological theory.

It should be understood that I am not denying that VOT is a phonetic fact; there is ample experimental evidence that the onset of voice is soonest in voiced sounds, later in voiceless unaspirated, and latest in voiceless aspirates. I am arguing that VOT is not what is represented in or manipulated by the phonology. The fact that differences in voice onset time exist does not allow us to conclude that this is crucial to phonology. In fact, just because the differences in timing exist, it does not logically follow that these are the crucial facts even for phonetic representation. Consider that when you aspirate a voiceless consonant, this happens on the release of the closure. Since the aspiration takes up some amount of time between the release and the onset of voicing, certainly the onset of voicing will be later than if you did nothing between the release and the voicing, instead of doing aspiration between the release and the voicing. VOT differences may be the result of doing something, and not the thing that is being done. I am not arguing that this is true in the phonetic representation; I am taking no stand on the phonetic representation of laryngeal distinctions. I am simply trying to make it clear that the VOT facts do not logically require that timing is the factor that is being manipulated, even in the phonetics, so these facts cannot be taken as evidence that this is the representation in the phonology.

Abramson (1977) argues that many later investigators have misunderstood and oversimplified the importance of the VOT phenomenon and Lisker and Abramson's claims for it. There are a number of interrelated phonetic cues for voicing (see for example Stevens and Klatt 1974, Lisker and Abramson 1970). Abramson argues that what is crucial to laryngeal distinctions is laryngeal timing, and that VOT is the utterance-initial manifestation of this. They used the voice onset measurement because it is an acoustic manifestation of laryngeal timing which it is possible to measure accurately, and never claimed that it was totally independent of other interrelated acoustic results of laryngeal timing. (Although Lisker (1975) argues that VOT is more important than formant transition, another frequently investigated perceptual cue to voicing.) Although I refer to VOT, my arguments apply to it as a theory of laryngeal timing regardless of the phonetic manifestation of laryngeal timing measured.

Differences in VOT and other facets of laryngeal timing are clearly the phonetic result and/or evidence of differences in underlying representation, since they serve to distinguish segments which differ in laryngeal features. But the evidence is overwhelming that the underlying *phonological* representation does not manipulate VOT or laryngeal timing (again, I make no claims about the phonetic representation). The arguments for this are presented below. A theory based on laryngeal timing cannot make the proper phonological distinctions in consonants, and therefore, it does not allow us to analyze the facts of laryngeal phonology in the world's languages. In the first place there are more than three phonologically distinctive phonation types; but more important, even adding the necessary features to the VOT system to describe these additional types, it does not predict the correct natural classes.

1.1.2.1 VOT and consonant systems: voiced aspirates. Consider the laryngeal contrasts made by the languages of the world, compared to the contrasts that can be made in a VOT framework. Glottalized consonants are not included in this system, and there are voiced and voiceless glottalized consonants. If voicing distinctions are a matter of voice onset, it would have to be shown that voice onset is shorter in voiced glottalized consonants than in voiceless glottalized consonants. This appears to be correct (Pinkerton 1986). However, we would then expect that the third, longest type of VOT could also combine with glottalization, but this does not happen: there are no aspirated glottalized consonants. Abramson (1977) says that laryngeal timing is involved in glottalized stops: timing between the closure of the vocal folds and the oral closure. However, no explanation of the cross-classification of glottalization and voicing is offered.

But even if glottalization is ignored, since VOT theory does not make a serious attempt to address this question, there is still a serious omission in the theory: the voiced aspirates (also called 'murmured' sounds). There is a good deal of data, both phonological and phonetic, that shows that these sounds are voiced and aspirated. The fact that VOT does not deal with these sounds is a major flaw, since voicing and aspiration are the very things it is a theory of.[3]

Some authors (for example, Ladefoged 1971) deny that voiced aspirates are aspirated sounds. (It should be noted that in later work (Ladefoged et. al. 1976, Ladefoged 1979) Ladefoged revises his view of aspiration and accepts that "voiced aspirated" is the correct characterization of these sounds.) This conflict exists both in traditional grammars and in the phonetic literature.[4] Although an explicit feature system is rarely used, a frequent assumption seems to be that "murmur" is some entirely separate phonation feature. There are a number of phonetic and phonological reasons that support the contention that these sounds are voiced and aspirated. The arguments come from patterning of consonant systems, phonetic evidence, and evidence from phonological rules.

The argument from patterning is that in general, languages that have the voiced aspirate also have voiced stops and aspirated stops; thus, considerations of markedness necessitate considering them to have the same feature for voice and the same feature for aspiration. The few exceptions can probably be explained as voiced sounds with unusual phonetic realizations.[5]

The weight of phonetic evidence also supports the contention that voiced aspirates have something in common with voiced sounds and something in common with aspirated sounds. Catford (1977) points out that Ladefoged objects to the use of the term "voiced aspirated" because it does not use either "voiced" or "aspirated" with the same meaning that they have elsewhere. But even if we assume delay in voice onset as the theory of aspiration, Catford notes that both voiced aspirated and voiceless aspirated stops involve a delay in the onset of *normal* voice; in the former, there is a period of whispery voice during the stop and for a certain time after the release. In addition, there is the same difference in intra-oral air pressure between the members of the pairs in voiced-voiced aspirated and voiceless-voiceless aspirated. (Catford, p113).

Dixit (1975; see also 1989), in a study of the phonetics of Hindi stops, makes the implicit assumption that voiced aspirates are parallel to voiceless aspirates. He claims that VOT is not actually similar for voiced and voiceless aspirates, but he says that there is a "long period of breathy voice" after a voiced aspirate (p.399) This is exactly Catford's point: Dixit is being particular about what a 'similar' VOT is, but the point is that it is longer for both of the aspirates than for the corresponding unaspirated sound. Since the state of the various parts of the larynx is not exactly the same due to the fact that one sound is voiced and one is not, we would not necessarily expect the exact same VOT, but the pattern of difference that is found is what is expected if a delay in voice onset is one of the results of aspiration.

Aside from VOT, Dixit shows various types of phonetic evidence of the expected correspondences: he finds that levels of muscle activity in the larynx correspond to the classes aspirated/unaspirated and voiced/voiceless, providing additional evidence that voiced aspirates are aspirates. The interarytenoid, lateral cricoarytenoid, and thyroarytenoid muscles show lower levels of activity for the aspirated class of consonants, and the cricothyroid muscle shows higher levels of activity for voiceless consonants (293 ff).

Another instrumental study is Yadav (1984) (also Ingemann and Yadav 1978). A fiberoptic study of Maithili stops, this work also finds the expected correspondences. Voicing correlates with adduction/abduction of the larynx; aspiration correlates with glottal width. The greatest glottal width is at or shortly after release. In voiced aspirates, the glottal opening is at the posterior, with cords continuing to vibrate throughout. Yadav argues from these results that glottal width is what is crucial to aspiration, and that VOT is just a consequence of this.[6]

Thus there is ample support for a phonetic argument that "murmured" sounds are voiced and aspirated. The confusion seems to have resulted from the fact that the definitions of what is crucial to aspiration have previously been made on the basis of evidence from languages that have voiced sounds and voiceless aspirates, but not voiced aspirates. Such languages would not provide the evidence needed to tease apart the factors responsible for the distinctions voiced/voiceless and aspirated/unaspirated.

However, since the object of this exercise is to arrive at a theory of phonological features, it is phonological evidence that should be given the greatest weight. The evidence above about phonological patterning is one type of phonological evidence, since it has to do with underlying phonological representation. Evidence from phonological rules also shows that aspiration should be marked with the same feature in voiced aspirates and voiceless aspirates. In chapter 3, the phonological evidence from neutralization shows that aspiration is marked with the same feature for voiced aspirates and voiceless aspirates: in languages where only aspiration is neutralized, they become plain voiced and voiceless. For example, Marathi (Houlihan and Iverson 1979) has final deaspiration, which applies to both voiced and voiceless aspirates:

(2)

tap	'fever'	tapala	'to the fever'
top	'cannon'	top^{h}ela	'to the cannon'
vad	'discussion'	vadala	'to the discussion'
dud	'milk'	dud^{h}ala	'to the milk'

Other languages with the same process are discussed in Chapter 3, supporting the claim that voiced and voiceless aspirates pattern together phonologically. More phonological evidence comes from the Tibeto-Burman language Limbu (Weidert and Subha 1985), where morphophonemic rules of voicing apply to plain voiceless and voiceless aspirated consonants, yielding voiced and voiced aspirated consonants. In Hindi (Ohala 1983) aspirated consonants cannot be the second consonant in stop-stop clusters; this includes both voiced and voiceless aspirates. The phonology of aspirated sonorants is discussed in chapter 4; the evidence from neutralization and other phonological rules supports marking these with the same feature as aspirated obstruents also.

I conclude that the evidence is clear that 'murmured' sounds should be marked voiced and aspirated. Abramson (1977) notes that voiced aspirates cannot be distinguished by VOT alone, and require an added dimension of glottal aperture. However, while this would allow a description of the sounds, it would not account for the fact that they pattern with voiceless aspirates phonetically and phonologically, since glottal aperture is not a feature of voiceless aspirates in their system. Thus the VOT framework fails in this important respect.

1.1.2.2 VOT and phonology. Since a fully detailed phonological theory using VOT for laryngeal contrasts has never been proposed, it is difficult to evaluate it. Consider two possible routes to take in creating a phonological theory based on VOT. One would be to represent the differences in timing directly in the phonological representation. This is attempted by Browman and Goldstein, discussed below. Another possibility would be to abstract away from the physical facts somewhat, and manipulate the scalar relationship of the three phonation types that the theory accounts for. We could represent this by giving each type a number in order:

(3)
```
   b    1
   p    2
   pʰ   3
```

This is more or less Ladefoged's (1973) proposal, where features are points along a continuum, designated by numbers, although he makes many more distinctions. If this is the relationship, the rules one can imagine acting on these representations would be the usual manipulations of integers, such as addition and subtraction, that would move the sounds to different points on the scale. This is not intrinsically absurd, since some rules of lenition do something that looks roughly like this. But in the case of laryngeal phonology examples of such rules do not give known phonological processes. For example, the rule that adds 1, or moves the sounds over one place on the scale has the following effect:

Add 1: b -> p, p -> pʰ, pʰ -> ?

This process does not exist in any known language; neither does the rule that subtracts 1:

Subtract 1: b -> ?, p -> b, pʰ -> p

And it is not clear how known phonological processes could be represented, for example syllable-final laryngeal neutralization whereby /p,pʰ,b/ all become [p], which as I have already mentioned is the most common phonological process involving the laryngeal features. One could represent this by a rule stipulating that all sounds change to the value 2 on the scale above. But this would not explain why neutralization always results in plain voiceless stops, because we could just as easily write a rule making all sounds change to some other value. It is also not clear how this theory could explain the fact that in languages with laryngeally marked sonorants, the result of neutralization is plain voiced sonorants. In the remainder of this study it will be shown that all of these facts can be given a principled explanation assuming a system of three privative laryngeal features and the basic mechanisms of autosegmental phonology and feature geometry.[7]

Current phonological theory does not use scales; the exception is the sonority hierarchy, but even this has been argued to be a result of binary features (Steriade 1982). Since laryngeal phonology can also be analyzed in terms of binary features, and since this scalar theory is inadequate in terms of representing known phonation types, there seems to be no reason to consider integrating such scalar devices into phonological theory.

The theory of Goldstein and Browman (1986, also Browman and Goldstein 1986) incorporates laryngeal timing as the means of representing laryngeal distinctions, in a theory of phonology based on the manipulation of the relative timing of different articulatory gestures. They do get one elegant result relating to voicing: The prohibition against [s]-voiced consonant clusters in English can be stated as: words can begin with at most one glottal gesture. [s] requires a glottal opening gesture; a following voiced consonant would require a closing gesture, but this is prohibited. Nonetheless it is still unclear that other aspects of laryngeal phonology, including the neutralization facts could be handled in this approach. In particular, the 'unmarked' state of the glottis in their theory is the state resulting in voiced stops, while the evidence from neutralization shows that the phonologically unmarked stop is voiceless. The difficulties for the VOT theory in the matter of voiced aspirates also remain. So for the moment the conclusion must stand that VOT is not a viable theory of the phonology of the laryngeal features.

1.1.3 Kingston's Articulatory Binding hypothesis

Another theory of laryngeal distinctions is that of Kingston (1985, 1990). Kingston's theory is that laryngeal distinctions are bound to the release of an obstruent, and that laryngeal distinctions will behave differently in sounds that have no release, that is, in fricatives and sonorants. Kingston (1990) states that this proposal, which he calls the binding hypothesis, is meant to account for two things:

1. The greater number and stability of glottal contrasts in stops as opposed to fricatives and sonorants,
2. The preferential alignment of glottal articulations in stops with the release rather than the closure.

A prediction of this theory is that in clusters, only the final, prevocalic stop will be distinctive for laryngeal features. This aspect of the theory will be discussed at the end of chapter 3. Here

I will address the other predictions of the theory. The crucial difficulty in this hypothesis is the prediction that fricatives will pattern with sonorants rather than obstruents, and I will concentrate on this.

The first point is the greater number of laryngeal contrasts in stops as opposed to fricatives and sonorants. In the case of sonorants this can be accounted for in part by the fact (see chapter 4) that since sonorants cannot bear the feature [voice], there are fewer possible types, since [voice] can cross-classify the other laryngeal features in obstruents but not in sonorants. Since there are fewer possible laryngeally marked sonorants, it is unsurprising that individual languages will have more types of stops than sonorants.

It also seems to be not uncommon for a language to have fewer laryngeal contrasts in fricatives than in stops. Part of this may be because aspirated fricatives are almost nonexistent, probably for phonetic or perceptual reasons, and glottalized fricatives are also rare. But this is not the whole explanation, since languages with a voicing contrast in stops often have only voiceless fricatives. Nonetheless, the question is whether the existence of fewer contrasts in fricatives and fewer contrasts in sonorants has the same cause in both cases. Certainly at least part of this is not susceptible to a generalization, since fricatives can be marked for voicing, unlike sonorants, and so the cross-classification explanation cannot be extended to sonorants. Sapir (1938) points out that in American languages, glottalized stops and affricates are most common; glottalized fricatives and sonorants are rarer, but glottalized sonorants are more common than glottalized fricatives. So in the matter of frequency, the generalization of fricatives and sonorants seems to be suspect.

Another aspect of this is what Kingston calls the 'stability' of these contrasts, meaning that glottal contrasts are more likely to be lost from sonorants and fricatives. (This is connected to the number of contrasts, since if these contrasts are easily lost from these segments, languages will tend to lose them from their inventories). He gives examples of the loss of glottalized sonorants in Wakashan languages. I do not attempt to explain historical change in laryngeal distinctions, and so since the goals of Kingston's work and mine differ here, I will not address this aspect of the theory. I will note however that the Wakashan example does not give any support to his claim that sonorants and fricatives pattern together, since there are no glottalized fricatives and he does not propose any connection between this and the loss of glottalized sonorants. His analysis of Yavapai also shows that obstruents and sonorants behave differently, but gives no evidence that fricatives pattern with sonorants.

A question that Kingston does not address is the fact that affricates tend to pattern with stops rather than fricatives with respect to laryngeal contrasts. Affricates often have the same system of laryngeal constrasts as the stops of a language, not the same system as the fricatives. Glottalized affricates are also more common than glottalized fricatives (see Maddieson 1984). Presumably the glottal contrast could be bound to the release of the stop portion of the affricate. Kingston does not propose a formalization of how the binding hypothesis should be incorporated into phonological representations, so it is not clear whether this solution is consistent with his theory.

The predictions of Kingston's theory that have to do with laryngeal features in consonant clusters are discussed at the end of chapter 3, where I show that the distribution of laryngeal features in clusters analyzed in chapters 2 and 3 cannot be accounted for by a theory based on release. His analysis of Klamath is discussed in the section of chapter 3 that deals with that language. Chapter 2, on voicing, and chapter 4, on sonorants, provide evidence that the natural classes with respect to the laryngeal feature of voice divide into obstruents vs. sonorants. The facts about neutralization in Tolowa (in chapter 4) also show that sonorants pattern with obstruents with respect to glottalization in that language.

Despite the evidence I present against Kingston's theory as a theory of the phonology of laryngeal distinctions, it should be kept in mind that the two goals of the theory quoted above are different from that of this study. His goals are largely concerned with explaining one point for which much of the evidence is historical, and one point that I would argue is mainly phonetic. This study does not make an attempt to explain those two points and I will not address the question of whether his theory meets those goals. For the same reasons I will not discuss the parts of Kingston (ms.) that address the nature of the consonants /h,?/, and that theorize that glottalized sonorants are complex segments similar to doubly articulated segments like labiovelars. Kingston's theory may provide explanations for these facts that I am not attempting to explain. However, as I will show in chapter 3, the binding hypothesis cannot be maintained as a theory of laryngeal distinctions in consonant clusters.

1.2 What laryngeal features are needed for phonology

The systems of Halle and Stevens and of Lisker and Abramson have one important thing in common: they both start from phonetic facts rather than phonological facts. What they both come up with, not surprisingly, is more like a system of phonetic features than phonological features. A system of phonological features should do two things: it should make all and only the contrasts that are found in the languages of the world, and it should group sounds into the natural classes that are actually found in phonological rules. A theory of phonetics has different goals: it should be able to distinguish the differences in realization in different languages. It will include properties of sounds that are never used distinctively. It will also have to include details that may be nondistinctive in the language in question although they are distinctive elsewhere. For instance, consider three languages. L1 and L2 each have one coronal stop; L3 has two coronal stops, an alveolar and a dental. The phonology of L3 must be able to distinguish between the alveolar and the dental; they must have different feature compositions to keep them apart in underlying representation, and possibly the language will have rules that treat them differently. Then, imagine that in L1 the coronal stop is dental, and in L2, alveolar. It seems to be a consensus in phonological theory that in both of these languages, the coronal is phonologically simply marked coronal; it does not have the additional features that mark the dental and alveolar in L3. The difference is confined to the phonetic realization rules that determine how [cor] is pronounced in L1 and in L2. A theory of phonetics should represent the fact that the coronals are dental in L1 and alveolar in L2, but a theory of phonology is only interested in the fact that they are coronal.

This reasoning also applies to the laryngeal features, but perhaps because these distinctions are perceived as more exotic, it rarely has been. Consider one case where it has been taken into account: It is often pointed out that voiced stops are pronounced differently in different languages. In some languages, voiced stops are slightly implosive. However, since this implosion is not phonologically distinctive, no one proposes that voiced stops in French should be marked anything other than [+voice]. A phonetic description of French would describe the difference between the pronunciation of English and French voiced stops, but a phonological description should not.

So to arrive at the correct system of features, we must examine the various phonation types that have been described in the literature. As noted earlier, Halle and Stevens describe 9 types. Ladefoged (1973) describes even more, 11, in his Table II. (4) gives the information from his table about examples of laryngeal distinctions in stops.

(4)

		Hausa	Korean	Hindi	Sindhi	Igbo	Uduk	Siswati	Beja
a	laryngealized (creaky voice)	x							x
a	voiced implosive				x	x	x		
b	voiced	x		x	x	x	x		x
c	voiceless lenis		x						
c	voiceless	x		x	x	x	x	x	x
d	murmured (breathy voiced)			x	x	x		x	x
e	aspirated		x	x	x	x	x	x	x
f	voiceless fortis		x						
f	voiceless ejective						x	x	
f	glottal stop plus stop								x
f	glottalic ingressive					x			

The sounds Ladefoged groups together with brackets are sounds that never contrast in a single language. Evidence for this can be found in other sources as well. Keating (1984) shows that voicing is realized differently in different languages, and argues that nevertheless phonological representations should not encode this. Dixit (1975) claims that voiceless unaspirated stops are produced differently in Hindi than they are in languages that have different stop series. Arguments for grouping the various types of voiced glottalized consonants as variants of one type of sound are also given in Greenberg (1970). Greenberg also concludes that only one glottalization feature is needed, arguing against a separate injective/ejective feature.[8] Lindau (1982), Pinkerton (1986) and Kingston (1985) show that glottalized consonants are realized differently in different languages.

Although Ladefoged indicates these groupings, he proposes a feature system that gives a separate characterization for all eleven sounds. Given the criteria I have described for a phonological feature system, his feature system is not phonological, then, although it may be a correct phonetic feature system. This is because the system makes more contrasts than are needed for phonological distinctions, which, as indicated by his bracketing, are only six contrasting phonation types:

(5)
    a. voiced glottalized (usually implosive)
    b. voiced
    c. voiceless
    d. voiced aspirate ("murmured")
    e. voiceless aspirated
    f. voiceless glottalized (usually ejective)

The six phonological phonation types in (5) demonstrate the point I have made earlier: that both aspiration and glottalization cross-classify voicing. The features needed to make these distinctions are three, which I will call [voice], [gl] and [asp]. I propose that these are privative features: they have no negative values. The possible combinations of these features are given in (6).[9]

(6) Laryngeal features of obstruents

	voice	gl	asp
voiceless			
voiced	+		
voiceless asp.			+
voiced asp.	+		+
voiceless gl.		+	
voiced gl.	+	+	

This chart shows that this three-feature system meets the first criterion for the adequacy of a feature system: that it makes all and only the necessary contrasts. The second criterion is that it makes the proper groupings for phonological rules. Above I have given some evidence of this for the combination of voicing and aspiration; the analyses in chapter 3 are additional evidence on this point as well as the evidence from aspiration and sonorants discussed in chapter 4.

The proposal that the laryngeal features are privative is necessary for a coherent theory of neutralization, as will be shown in the following chapters. This claim is relatively unproblematic for [gl] and [asp]. It is more or less the informal practice of phonologists, since for example unaspirated sounds are almost never marked [-asp] in analyses, and I have found no cases where the negative values of these features are needed for a phonological analysis[10]. There is also positive evidence for the absence of the negative values: for example, there are cooccurrence restrictions on glottalized consonants (for example in various Mayan languages; see Lombardi 1990b for some examples) and none on nonglottalized consonants. [voice] as a privative feature is more controversial; Chapter 2 gives extensive arguments for this position.

The chart above applies only to obstruents. In Chapter 4 I discuss the phonology of sonorants. There is strong evidence that sonorants are not phonologically marked [voice]. They can be marked [gl] or [asp]. Greenberg points out that sonorants can only have one glottalized series, unlike obstruents. I would argue that this is additional evidence that [voice] is the feature that distinguishes the two types of glottalized obstruents. Since sonorants cannot be marked [voice], they cannot be marked [voice, gl]. Thus there is only one possible type of glottalized sonorant, one marked only [gl]. The possible laryngeal markings for sonorants, then, are as given in (7):

(7) Laryngeal features of sonorants

	gl	asp
voiced		
aspirated,"voiceless"		+
glottalized	+	

Chapter 4 gives evidence that sonorants described as voiceless are phonologically aspirated.

My assumptions about the geometry of the laryngeal features follow Clements (1985)[11]: that there is a Laryngeal node dependent upon the Root node, and the Laryngeal features are sisters under the Laryngeal node. Additional support for the nodelike behavior of the laryngeal features can be found mainly in chapter 3. I have not found sufficient phonological evidence to propose any further structure or dependency within the Laryngeal node. It is somewhat suggestive that while there is neutralization of aspiration without neutralization of voicing, I have not found neutralization of voicing without neutralization of aspiration. This might suggest that [asp] is dependent upon [voice]. However, the evidence does not require this and is not sufficient to support this proposal. Evidence from spreading is hard to come by; I give evidence in chapter 3 that the entire Laryngeal node of voiced aspirates spreads in some languages, but I have not found spreading of aspiration (or glottalization) without spreading of voice. Proposing a dependency relationship would also be theoretically problematic. In other cases in the current framework of feature geometry that I am assuming, a dependent feature cannot appear in the absence of its dominating feature: for instance, only coronals can bear [ant]. It is clearly not true that only voiced sounds can be aspirated, so if [asp] were dependent on [voice] the meaning of such dependency would be inconsistent.

Notes

1. This work will not deal with the question of the interaction of tone and consonantal phonation types. For a critique of the Halle and Stevens system treatment of tone, see Anderson (1978).

2. Hayes (1984) uses the features to analyze the behavior of [v/f] in Russian voicing assimilation. The issue is that it has been claimed that this sound acts sometimes like an obstruent and sometimes like a sonorant. Briefly, the problem is that it behaves like a sonorant in voicing assimilation, but is voiceless word-finally and surfaces as a sound that is generally considered an obstruent. Various authors give conflicting data, but Coats and Harshenin (1971) give evidence that this sound has the same behavior as other sonorants in Russian, including with respect to final devoicing. They also refer to phonetic studies that suggest that this sound is sonorant on the surface, and is not identical to, for example, English [v]. If in fact the sound in question is simply a labiodental sonorant, the analysis is basically that given for the Polish data in chapter 2 below.

Lisker and Abramson present their arguments against the Halle and Stevens system in Lisker and Abramson (1971).

3. Lisker and Abramson (1964) do examine some languages with voiced aspirates. They note that difference in VOT are "almost systematic" but ranges are "nearly coextensive", and conclude that voiced aspirates are distinguished from plain voiced sounds by "low amplitude buzz mixed with noise in the interval following release of the stop". These results are of little use in arriving at a system of phonological features. Abramson's (1977) later remarks on voiced aspirates are discussed below.

4. Although native grammars usually consider them voiced aspirates; this seems to be the clear native intuition. The Sanskrit grammarians definitely considered these sounds to have voice and aspiration; see Allen (1953).

5. Another possible exception is Proto-Indo-European. PIE is traditionally reconstructed as having voiced, voiceless, and voiced aspirated consonants. This system is unknown in any living

language. Hopper (1973) argues for an alternate reconstruction that includes voiceless, ejective, and murmured. Unfortunately this system is also unknown, and his ideas as to what 'murmur' is demonstrate some confusion over the nature of these sounds. In fact most of his arguments are consistent with the assumption that the third series is plain voiced, and this would give a commonly known consonant system. In any case, since we should reject any reconstruction of PIE that results in a consonant system unknown in human languages, PIE should not be considered an exception to the generalization I am making. See Collinge (1985, Appendix II) for a survey of recent re-reconstructions.

6. Yadav's position, then, is that VOT is not what is manipulated by the phonetics. If this is correct and VOT is not part of the phonetic representation it seems even less likely that it is part of the underlying phonological representation.

Possible additional evidence comes from Maddieson and Gandour (1977): in Hindi, vowels are shortest before voiceless unaspirates, next longest before voiceless aspirates and voiced sounds, and longest before voiced aspirates. They say there is a rule that adds one increment of length before aspirates and one increment of length before voiced sounds; thus a sound that is voiced and aspirated has two increments. While I do not see how to adapt this analysis to the phonological framework I am assuming, the facts are of interest in this context.

7. Some readers have commented that it would be fairer to the VOT idea to number the sounds as in (a), rather than as in (b), which is the system in the text:
    a. $b\ {-}1$ $p\ 0$ $p^h\ 1$
    b. $b\ 1$ $p\ 2$ $p^h\ 3$

But this obscures the point that /p/ is *not* the unmarked position in this system; simply calling it zero does not make it so. If we allow only addition and subtraction, in neither system can we write a single rule that neutralizes all three sounds to /p/.

We could make use of the privileged status of /p/=0 if we allow multiplication as well as addition. Then laryngeal neutralization is:
    a. $Z = 0 \times Y$ Will result in 0 for $Y = -1, 0$ or 1

But if we allow multiplication, presumably we can combine it with addition, if both operations are required. Then we can also can write an equation that results in /p/ in the (b) system:

b. $Z = 2 + (0 \times Y)$ Will result in 2 for $Y = 1, 2$ or 3

In the (b) system we can change this equation so that it results in any other sound on the scale, giving rules of neutralization to /b/ or /pʰ/:

b. $Z = 1 + (0 \times Y)$ Will result in 1 for $Y = 1, 2$ or 3
$Z = 3 + (0 \times Y)$ Will result in 3 for $Y = 1, 2$ or 3

This might make it seem like the (a) system is less arbitrary, since we cannot replace 0 in that equation with other numbers on the scale and get different neutralization rules. But what we get is simply several different types of nonexistent rules instead. In fact multiplication alone allows us to write many nonexistent rules in the (a) system, such as:

a. $Z = -1 \times Y$

Thus the (a) system is no improvement and does not allow us to use VOT as a coherent theory of laryngeal phonology: Only if we allow multiplication can we get a rule of neutralization to /p/, but then we predict a even larger number of nonexistent phonological processes than if we only allow addition and subtraction.

8. Greenberg concludes that glottalization must cross-classify a tense/lax distinction rather than [voice], because voiceless injective stops are reported for some languages. However, this can be considered simply another possible realization of voiceless glottalized consonants (as Ladefoged groups it above). There is no evidence that voiceless injectives and voiceless ejectives should be distinguished phonologically. Greenberg mentions voiceless injectives in several languages, such as the Mayan languages Aguatec, Chontal and Pomochi, but these are all allophones, not phonemic contrasts. I have not seen the description of the Caucasian language Andi, which he says has ejectives differing by fortis/lenis and not voicing.

9. Mathematically we would expect two more possibilities. However, these last two combinations of features would give sounds that are marked [gl] and [asp] at the same time. Glottalization involves a constriction of the glottis, and aspiration

(recall Yadav 1984, for example) involves spreading of the glottis, and it is physically impossible to do both at the same time.

10. Steriade (1982) gives an analysis of Greek consonant clusters which employs double linking of [-asp]. This data is reanalyzed in chapter 3.

11. The idea that the laryngeal features are dominated by a class node was proposed earlier by Mascaro (1983) and Mohanon (1983).

CHAPTER 2

THE FEATURE [VOICE] AND VOICING ASSIMILATION

2.1 Introduction

The feature [voice] is usually assumed to be binary, because there are many cases where both values of [voice] appear to assimilate. However, current phonological theory also frequently invokes the unmarked status of voiceless sounds. For example, Clements (1985) argues for grouping the laryngeal features under a distinct node by appealing to the phenomenon of laryngeal neutralization: in Thai the distinction voiced, aspirated and voiceless unaspirated is neutralized word-finally to voiceless unaspirated, and Clements analyzes this as delinking of the entire Laryngeal node. The crucial assumption in this analysis is that a sound with no laryngeal features--the result of delinking the entire node--is voiceless.

Such an analysis is at odds with the assumption that [voice] is a binary feature. It would be preferable not to have two ways to represent voiceless sounds--as marked [-voice], or as unmarked-- unless it could be demonstrated that the two representations exhibit different phonological properties. In addition, there is evidence in favor of the nonexistence of the feature value [-voice]. For example, there are known cooccurrence restrictions on [voice] (for example, in Japanese, discussed in chapter 4) but I know of no such restrictions on [-voice].

This inconsistency can be resolved if it can be shown that [voice] is a privative feature. This goal can be achieved by making a connection between the two facts noted about voicelessness: that neutralization yields voiceless sounds, and that voicelessness appears to spread. I will argue that assimilation of [voice] is a two part process consisting of neutralization of [voice] and spreading of [voice], and that the 'assimilation' of voicelessness is simply a result of the first part of the process, neutralization.

Such an analysis of voice assimilation was suggested by Mester and Ito (1989), which outlines some of the issues that the analysis must deal with.

Mester and Ito (1989) discuss Lyman's Law in Japanese, which prohibits two voiced obstruents in a morpheme. It also blocks the application of Rendaku, a rule that voices the initial obstruent of the second member of a compound. Intervening voiceless obstruents do not block Lyman's Law. This is a problem for the theory of Restricted Underspecification for which Mester and Ito are arguing. In such a theory, since there is a voicing contrast in obstruents, both [+voice] and [-voice] should be underlyingly specified. If [-voice] is underlying, then the [+voice] specifications of obstruents would not be adjacent. However, Lyman's Law shows that they behave as if phonologically adjacent. Mester and Ito argue that if [voice] is a privative feature, the correct results for Lyman's Law can be achieved while still preserving the theory of Restricted Underspecification.

If [voice] is privative in Japanese, ideally this should be true universally, since the more restrictive theory is one in which languages do not have the option of having a feature be either privative or binary. In order to show that [voice] is privative, the following must be proven:

1. Segments are not underlyingly marked [-voice].
2. [-voice] is never active in the phonology.

These two statements have a number of consequences. Mester and Ito point out that a consequence of the first statement is that there can be no underlyingly voiceless sonorants; they argue that such cases can be analyzed as marked as aspirated, not voiceless. I will argue for this in detail in chapter 4.

The consequence of the second point is that it must be possible to reanalyze those cases of phonological processes that have been traditionally analyzed as crucially involving reference to [-voice]. There are two such cases: dissimilation of [-voice] in Dahl's Law in Bantu, and the many well-known cases of assimilation of [-voice]. The first phenomenon is quite rare; I will return to this later. Assimilation is quite common, however, and a successful analysis of it is crucial to the privative voicing theory.

Mester and Ito suggest that apparent assimilation of [-voice] can be handled by assuming "the classic Praguean conception of the relation between neutralization and assimilation" that "conceives of all unmarked assimilation process as contingent on prior neutralization." ("Unmarked" here means the negative value of a feature such as [voice].) They suggest that in Russian, for example, the analysis of voicing assimilation is as follows:
  1. Nonprevocalic obstruents lose their laryngeal nodes.
  2. [voice] spreads to the left.
Thus, if the rightmost, prevocalic consonant is voiced, the feature [voice] will spread, yielding a cluster of all voiced consonants. If the rightmost consonant is voiceless, there is no feature to spread; but the result is exactly the correct one, a cluster of all voiceless consonants. This gives the effect that all clusters agree in voicing, with no need for a feature value [-voice].

As it stands, however, Mester and Ito's analysis is only a suggestion; many details remain to be worked out. A central issue is the exact nature of the neutralization process--in particular, what is the domain of neutralization. There are many possibilities. For Russian, Mester and Ito refer to non-prevocalic consonants. Languages such as German are traditionally described as having syllable-final neutralization. Kingston (1985, 1990) suggests that only prevocalic stops can bear laryngeal distinctions because only these are released. Cho (1990a,b) proposes that languages can have coda-delinking, word-final delinking, or delinking in clusters.

I will analyze neutralization as the result of a positive well-formedness condition of licensing of segment content in a particular syllable configuration. The next section will begin with an outline of the theory of neutralization and spreading that I am proposing. I will outline the mechanisms of the theory briefly and give a sample analysis of Dutch for a demonstration of how the mechanisms of the theory work, with a brief mention of German and Yiddish. Section 2.2 gives detailed analysis of a number of languages. Section 2.3 examines the predictions of the theory, and compares it to other possible theories of neutralization. Section 2.4 examines other possible counterexamples to the theory of privative voicing: dissimilation of [-voice].

2.1.1 Overview of the theory

In this section I present first a list of the premises and mechanisms of the theory. These mechanisms are those which are required to explain the most common cross-linguistic patterns of voice neutralization and assimilation. Then I present a brief analysis of Dutch, with some reference to other languages, as a simple exemplification of the way these mechanisms work. The following sections will then analyze a number of languages in detail, including language-specific laryngeal phonology where necessary.

The basic points of the theory are as follows:

1. [voice] is a privative feature. Voiceless obstruents have no marking for laryngeal features. I argue that the proper representation is one with no Laryngeal node. The factual support for this is mainly to be found in the next chapter which deals with languages with multiple laryngeal distinctions, since it is difficult to demonstrate the behavior of a node unless more than one feature is dominated by it. The argument is as follows:

i. There is no phonological contrast between a representation with a bare Laryngeal node and no Laryngeal node at all. Therefore any theory should allow only one type of representation.

ii. The usefulness of the Laryngeal node, like any node, is that it allows us to explain why groups of features pattern together. In the case of the Laryngeal node, the most obvious case is final neutralization of multiple Laryngeal contrasts, which results in a voiceless sound (see chapter 3). To get the benefit of having a Laryngeal node in the theory, we must analyze this as delinking of the entire node (the alternative being to delinking each feature individually, which loses the generalization). This leaves a sound with no Laryngeal node, so this is the correct representation for voiceless sounds.

2. Languages that have neutralization have the following positive licensing constraint: [voice] is only licensed in an obstruent if it stands before a [+son] segment in the same syllable.[1] I will call this the Voice Constraint for the moment, and the licensed configuration is as given in (1). In Chapter 3, the

formulation of the constraint will be refined and extended to other laryngeal features.

(1)
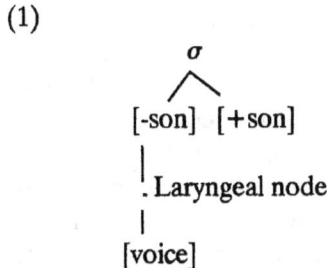

[+son] includes both vowels and sonorants (I am assuming following Clements (1987) that major class features are never underspecified.) Thus, voiced obstruents can appear in the configurations in (2a) and (2b).

(2) a.

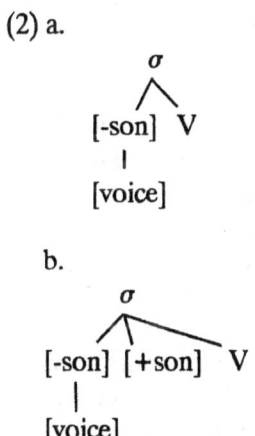

b.

The licensing of a feature in this way is an extension of the idea of Prosodic Licensing, which requires that phonological units belong to higher levels of prosodic structure (Ito 1986, Goldsmith 1990). The reasons that this must be stated as a positive rather than a negative constraint will be explored in section 2.3.1, where I compare this theory to other possible theories of neutralization. The behavior of linked structures with respect to this constraint is a crucial aspect of the theory; this will be discussed in the outline of Dutch voicing assimilation below.

3. Spreading. Languages can have a specific rule, Spread [voice]. I will also argue for a related process of Fusion that also creates linked [voice] structures. The spreading rule will be referred to as spreading of [voice] in this chapter, but actually consists of spreading the Laryngeal node, consistent with the statement above that voiceless sounds have no Laryngeal node (and thus no node for [voice] to spread to, if it were spread of a single feature.) Again, more evidence for this formulation is to be found in chapter 3, since it is not possible to demonstrate the behavior of a node when only one dependent feature is involved. There it will be shown that there is spreading of the entire Laryngeal node in some cases. There is no contrast between spreading a single feature and spreading a node dominating a single feature, and I have shown that we must analyze delinking as delinking of the entire node. Thus, spread of [voice], rather than spread of that single feature, is actually spread of the Laryngeal node to a sound with no Laryngeal node of its own.

4. Final consonant exceptionality. The Voice Constraint will cause word-final neutralization of [voice]. But there are languages that give evidence of word-internal neutralization that do not have word-final neutralization, such as Yiddish, Romanian, and Serbo-Croatian. In such languages, final consonants escape the constraint. (See the end of this section for more discussion.)

5. Another fact about voicing that will be important in some cases, mentioned by Mester and Ito (1989), was noted by Harms (1973) and Greenberg (1978). Voiced obstruents are more sonorous than voiceless, therefore the following configurations are impossible within a syllable:
 *syllable nucleus-voiceless obstruent-voiced obstruent
  e.g. Vsd
 *voiced obstruent-voiceless obstruent-syllable nucleus
  e.g. sdV

I will refer to this as the Universal Sonority constraint.

The Feature [voice] and Voicing Assimilation

With these mechanisms, voicing assimilation can be analyzed without recourse to a feature [-voice]. Consider the following somewhat simplified analysis of Dutch (Mascaro ms., van der Hulst 1980, Berendsen 1983. The full range of data requires additional rules that will be discussed later.)

(3)
    a. hui[z]en   'houses'
    b. hui[s]   'house'
    c. hui[sk]ammer   'livingroom'
    d. hui[zb]aas   'landlord'
    e. kra[b]en   'to scratch'
    f. kra[p]   'scratch'
    g. kra[ps]el   'scratchings'
    h. zi[db]ad   'hipbath'
    i. zitten   'sit'

Dutch has the Voice Constraint and spreading of [voice]. Recall that the constraint means that [voice] can only appear a consonant before a vowel (or sonorant) in the same syllable. Word-final consonants as in (3b) will be voiceless, then, since [voice] linked to a word final consonant is not in this configuration and would be unlicensed, and consequently delinks.

Spreading of [voice] is shown in (3h). The underlying form is *zi[tb]ad*; [voice] spreads from [b] to the unmarked [t], yielding a syllable-final [d]. Ordinarily a syllable-final voiced stop would be a violation of the constraint, and [voice] would delink. What is crucial here is the fact that spreading creates a linked structure, as in (4):

(4)
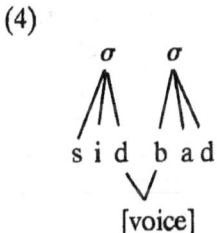

In this representation, [voice] is licensed because of its association to /b/, which is in the correct configuration. /d/ is not in the licensed position, but the [voice] that it is associated to is already licensed. Thus /d/ can be voiced, since no constraint on the representation is violated; all association lines that are required by the Voice Constraint are present. I will refer to this effect of linking as Parasitic Licensing.

Ito adopts Hayes's Linking Condition (1986) to account for linking effects. Most of the constraints she discusses are stated as negative constraints, but her theory predicts linking effects with both positive and negative constraints, which is what would be expected given the formal equivalence of positive and negative constraints. If we had the formally equivalent negative constraint that ruled out [voice] in the coda, (4) would be well-formed. It is to be expected, then, that if the positive constraint is formally equivalent, it should have the same effects as the negative constraint, and the representation in (4) should be well-formed.

But if we examine the behavior of positive constraints such as the Voice Constraint with respect to multiple linking, it seems that the Linking Condition and its relatives are not the correct way to account to these effects. It is not correct that *any* doubly linked [voice] structure escapes the Voice Constraint; at least one consonant must be in the properly licensed configuration. (5) is not possible in Dutch:

(5)

$$
\begin{array}{cc}
\sigma & \sigma \\
\bigtriangleup & \bigtriangleup \\
\text{*sidz} & \text{pad} \\
& \diagdown\diagup \\
& \text{[voice]}
\end{array}
$$

Thus the effect in (4) cannot be explained as due to the Linking Condition, which would predict that (5) would escape the constraint. Selkirk (1990a,b) argues that effects of multiple linking should not be accounted for by conditions such as the Linking Condition (Hayes 1986) or the Uniform Applicability Condition (Schein and Steriade 1986) but rather follow from conditions on the wellformedness of multiply linked structures. If there is no Linking Condition, (5) is not expected to be well-formed. Thus (5) violates the constraint because [voice] is not in the licensed configuration; (4) does not violate it, as [voice] is licensed, and the additional association line has no effect.

Word-internal consonants that do not precede a vowel will also be subject to the constraint. The derivation of (3c), then is as follows:

(6)
    underlying form   hui[z k]ammer
    delinking of
    unlicensed [voice]   hui[s k]ammer

("Delinking of unlicensed [voice]" will henceforth be referred to simply as "neutralization".) The result of this is that the cluster is uniformly voiceless, without spreading of a negative value of [voice]. While Dutch does have Spreading of [voice], it does not apply here, since /k/ has no [voice] to spread.

Neutralization will also produce uniformly voiceless word-final clusters, as in (7):

(7)
    a. kie[z]en   'to choose'
    b. kie[st]   'he chooses'

Underlying [z] will lose voicing when [t] is suffixed, just like when it is final, since it violates the constraint.

Given that word-internal consonants are subject to the Constraint, the most obvious analysis of voiced clusters such as the one in (3d) is that there is neutralization, and revoicing via spread of [voice]:

(8)
    u.f.:   hui[zb]aas
    neutralization: hui[sb]aas
    spread: hui[zb]aas

In a more detailed analysis of Dutch that follows I will present evidence that this rather futile devoicing and revoicing does not in fact take place: rather, that [voice] specifications that become adjacent fuse into one linked structure, which is parasitically licensed just like the structure created by spreading.

It should be noted that the two-step process of delinking and spread proposed in this theory is not a disadvantage when comparing it to the theory in which both values of binary [voice] spread. If the latter theory is made explicit, spreading must be preceded by delinking also; in fact, *all* derivations will have these two steps, including those that only require one step under the privative theory. Consider the derivation of (3h) in such a theory. Assuming a theory of restricted underspecification as argued for by Mester and Ito (1990), the relevant part of the underlying form will be as given in (9), because as there is a contrast of voicing in the obstruents, both values of [voice] would be specified underlyingly. It is obvious that in order for [+voice] to spread, [-voice] must delink:

(9)
UR: si t   b a d
    ǂ˗˗˗˷|
    [-voice] [+voice]

A theory of radical underspecification with binary [voice] would also require some kind of delinking or neutralization. If there is no [-voice] in the representation because it is underspecified, it cannot spread; the effect of spreading of [-voice] will have to be achieved by neutralization, as in the privative theory. If we assume that redundant values are filled in before rules mention them as in Archangeli's Redundancy Rule Ordering Constraint (Archangeli 1984), the relevant representation will be the same as the one in (9). Thus, regardless of what other assumptions are made, the binary [voice] theory has no advantage of simplicity over a neutralization and spreading account, since it must also include a delinking step prior to spreading.

Dutch is an example of the familiar case in which assimilation correlates with word-final devoicing. A case such as German, with syllable-final devoicing, is identical to Dutch except that the rule of Spreading is absent: the Voice Constraint will cause delinking of [voice] from all syllable-final consonants, since syllable-final consonants are not in the position licensed by the Constraint.

Another possibility is a language like Yiddish, in which there is assimilation in word-internal clusters, but no word-final devoicing. In the present framework, this means that the language must have the Voice Constraint, because assimilation in clusters is a result of the Voice Constraint and spreading. But the Voice Constraint would also cause word-final consonants to devoice.

Yiddish, then is an example of a language with Final Exceptionality: word-final consonants escape the constraint. The mechanism of final exceptionality is an extension idea of final extrametricality: Phonological theory recognizes the fact that constituents at word edges can have different behavior from their word-internal counterparts. For instance, word final syllables can include final elements that are not allowed in word-internal syllables; word-final syllables can act as though their final elements are not present for the purpose of stress rules. The idea of Final Exceptionality as applied to the Voice Constraint is that this kind of word-final exceptionality is also possible at the segmental level. As segments can be invisible to rules mentioning higher levels of structure (syllables), features can be invisible to rules mentioning higher levels of structure (segments). Thus, [voice] can appear at word-edges, escaping the constraint, by final "extrametricality". In Section 2.3 I will show that the correct predictions are made by allowing this kind of word-edge exceptionality.

Because the Voice Constraint is a positive constraint, its behavior is somewhat different than the more familiar negative constraints (see for example the discussion above of the Linking Condition). Is this the case here as well? Extrametricality generally blocks a negative constraint from applying; an item that would normally be prohibited is exempt from the constraint. In the Voice Constraint cases, the effect is basically the same. [voice] on final consonants would normally be prohibited, as it would be unlicensed; in cases with Final Exceptionality, the normally unlicensed element is allowed to remain. Negative constraints are descriptions of what is unlicensed in a particular position; positive constraints describe what is licensed in a particular position. In the case of word-edge exceptions, unlicensed elements are allowed to remain; this is the same regardless of the type of constraint involved.

2.2 Analyses

2.2.1 Languages with Neutralization and Spread

2.2.1.1 Dutch. The partial analysis of Dutch takes into consideration only clusters composed entirely of stops. Fricatives are subject to additional rules. The following data from van der Hulst (1980) gives the possible combinations (in all cases there is a morpheme boundary between the two consonants):

(10)
a. stofzak   [fs]
   slaapzak   [ps]
b. huizvuil   [sf]
   hebzucht   [ps]
c. asbak   [zb]
   zakdoek   [gd]
d. kasboek   [zb]
   bedbank   [db]
e. leezfout   [sf]
   kaazkop   [sk]
   braadpan   [tp]
f. bosfee   [sf]
   waskaars   [sk]
   pakpaard   [kp]

The rules already given accounts for the examples in (10c-f). In (10c), spreading of [voice] applies; in (10d) neutralization and spreading; in (10e) neutralization; and in (10f) two voiceless consonants come together, and no rules are needed.

In (10a-b) the rules already given would predict voiced clusters, but the clusters are voiceless. This is usually analyzed as a rule of progressive assimilation of [-voice] applying when the second consonant is a fricative (van der Hulst 1980, Berendsen 1983). In such an analysis, if assimilation follows a rule of syllable-final devoicing, the fricative will get the value [-voice] from the devoiced consonant. This analysis can be restated in terms of the present framework by including a language-specific rule of Progressive Neutralization:

(11)
$$[-son] \quad [-son, +cont]$$
$$\not{+}$$
$$[voice]$$

This rule must apply before the spreading of [voice], presuming that the linked structure created by spreading would be immune to this rule due to the Linking Condition. (This ordering will follow from the Elsewhere Condition.) This rule alone applies in (10a), and this rule preceded by the usual neutralization produced by the Voice Constraint applies in (10b).

Another issue that must be examined in more detail has to do with examples like (8), repeated here:

(12)
```
u.f.:            hui[zb]aas
neutralization:  hui[sb]aas
spread:          hui[zb]aas
```

This is the obvious derivation, but I will present evidence that neutralization and spread do not have to take place here--that clusters that already agree do not undergo devoicing and revoicing. This evidence comes from the Dutch past tense morpheme. This morpheme shows progressive assimilation like fricatives, although it is a stop on the surface (data from Berendsen 1983).

(13)
a. kra[bd]e   'scratch'   b. schra[pt]e 'scrape'
   bloe[dd]e   'bleed'   haa[tt]e   'hate'
   schaa[vd]e   'plane'   bla[ft]e   'bark'
   vee[ɣd]e   'stroke'   la[xt]e   'laugh'

c. skide   'ski'
   talmde   'hesitate'
   broeide   'heat'
   breide   'knit'

Berendsen (1983), following Trommelen and Zonneveld (1982), assumes that the past-tense suffix is fricative-initial underlyingly, and is hardened to a stop. He shows that if we also assume that Dutch weak verbs have an underlying final vowel that does not surface (following Zonneveld 1982), these forms can be correctly derived with a syllable-final devoicing rule. Translating this analysis into the present framework, the derivations are as in (14).

(14)
   a.   la.[xə.ðə]
   Voice constraint   no effect: all [voice]
                                 is licensed
   Vowel deletion   la [x ðə]
   Progressive Neut.   la [x θə]
   Spread   no effect
   Strengthening   la[xtə]

   b.   schra[pə.ðə]
   voice constraint   no effect
   vowel deletion   schra[p .ðə]
   Progressive Neut.   schra[p θə]
   Spread   no effect
   strengthening   schra[ptə]

The derivation of [krabde] calls for additional comment:

   c.   kra.[bə.ðə]
   Voice Constraint   no effect
   Vowel deletion   kra.[b ðə]

At this point, [b] is in a position that is unlicensed. But we cannot allow it to devoice and rely on Spread to voice it again-- Progressive Neutralization will devoice the fricative before it can spread its [voice] to the left. How is it that this surfaces as a voiced cluster?

      The effects of Parasitic Licensing are crucial to all of these analyses of voicing assimilation. In a language with the Voice Constraint, something like #dV is licensed, and something like #zdV is also licensed: the cluster is linked to one [voice] specification, and because the second consonant is in the licensed position, the first consonant is parastically licensed. In [krabde], two voiced consonants come together, and there is no devoicing.

This would be expected if the two consonants immediately become doubly linked for [voice]--if the OCP fuses the adjacent identical laryngeal nodes. (This is similar to the Fusion of identical segments to form geminates, simultaneous with morpheme concatenation, proposed by Ito 1986, p 138.)

An immediate objection would be a language with final devoicing and no spreading--for example a form like German *rund+gang* -> *runtgang* (see below, section 2.2.2). If the two voiced consonants fused, it would be impossible for neutralization to apply to [d]. But there is a crucial difference between the two languages: Dutch has spreading of [voice] and German does not. Thus there is a correlation: a language with spreading (Dutch) gives evidence of having fusion; a language without spreading (German) does not have fusion.

The OCP would presumably disallow adjacent [voice] specifications. But in a language like Dutch, linked [voice] structures are acceptable. Imagine that the OCP fuses the adjacent identical laryngeal nodes, when two voiced consonants become adjacent. This allows the analysis of the past tense *krabde*. It also means that clusters of two underlyingly voiced consonants do not have to devoice by Neutralization and revoice by Spread, a result with undeniable aesthetic appeal.

Fusion is impossible in German, a language where linked [voice] structures are impossible. Thus, adjacent voiced consonants do not undergo fusion, and are not protected from neutralization; the syllable-final consonant will undergo devoicing, the correct result.

Fusion and Spreading are not the same process, however. The past tense of [krabde] shows that Fusion must apply before Progressive Neutralization, and the derivations in (14) show that Spreading applies after Progressive Neutralization. The two processes are connected by the fact that they both occur in languages that allow multiply linked [voice], but are not the same. Fusion is a result of well-formedness conditions in such a language--it is the immediate result of OCP violations, fusing identical nodes. Spreading is a separate rule, because its description is different: it is the spreading of the laryngeal node to segments without such a node.

One last point remains in the analysis of Dutch. If laryngeal nodes fuse automatically and the linked structure escapes the

Voice Constraint, how can Progressive Assimilation apply in a form like (10b), *hui[zv]uil -> [sf]*? Recall that all of those forms are compounds. [z] has already devoiced before the level of compounding; morpheme-final obstruents are voiceless in a compound even when the second member is vowel-initial:

(15) huid # arts -> hui[t]arts

So there is no point in the derivation of (10b) where two voiced consonants come together, and so no Fusion. Progressve Neutralization will apply to the second consonant in the cluster, since it is a fricative following an obstruent.

2.2.1.2 Catalan. Catalan also has voicing agreement in medial consonant clusters, and word-final devoicing. The basic analysis is therefore identical to Dutch.

(16)
    a. me[z]os   'months'
       me[s]   'month'
       me[s k]urt 'short month'
       me[z ß]inent 'next month'
    b. dece[ß]edor 'deceptive' (underlying [b])
       perce[p]   'perceives'
       perce[p s]io 'perception'

Catalan also has some additional facts that confirm the importance of syllable structure in the constraint: the constraint cannot simply be stated as licensing [voice] before a sonorant, but must refer to the syllable constituency as well. As seen in (17c) below, both [bl] and [pl] are possible syllable onsets. However, the sequence stressed vowel/labial stop/[l] will almost always be [Vpl], although [bl] is possible when the preceding vowel is unstressed (17b): (examples from Mascaro 1976, ms.)[2]

(17)
   a. kóplə   'music band'
      répla   'feeble'
      əstáplə   'stable'
   b. ublík   'oblique'
      ublidá   'to forget'
   c. sƐm.blə 'it seems'
      tem.plə   'temple'

This generalization also holds of labials that are underlyingly voiced:

(18)
a.		b.	
mɔplə	'item of furniture'	mubilyári	'furniture'
diáplə	'devil'	diəbɔlik	'devilish'
pusípla	'possible'	pusibilitát	'possibility'
bukáplə	'word'	bukəbulári	'vocabulary'

It seems likely that the labial consonants in (17a) and (18a) are part of the preceding stressed syllable, possibly because the stressed syllable must be heavy. Thus they are syllable-final; although they precede a sonorant, they do not have the syllabic association required by the constraint. If the Voice Constraint referred only to linear order, there would be no way to account for these facts; it would be predicted that these consonants would remain voiced. Although the present theory does not have a rule of syllable-final neutralization, syllable constituency is still crucial to it. The fact that [voice] is licensed only in the particular syllable configuration in the constraint is what gives the surface effect that has been described as syllable-final devoicing.

2.2.1.3 Polish. In consonant sequences in Polish all obstruents agree in voicing. Initial and medial clusters can be voiced (19) or voiceless (20). (Data from Gussmann ms., Bethin 1989.)[3]

(19)
  a. [gd]y   'when'
     [db]ać   'take care'
     [bzd]ura   'nonsense'
     [dždž]ownica 'earthworm'

  b. o[dg]rodzić   'separate'
     gwia[zd]a   'star'
     o[dvz]ajemić 'reciprocate'

(20)
  a. [pt]ak   'bird'
     [kt]o   'who'
     [pštš]ołₐ   'bee'
     [pst]ry   'gaudy'

  b. ne[ptk]a   'twit, gen.sg.'
     pa[štš]a   'gorge'
     gwia[stk]a   'star, dim.'
     o[tst]raszyć 'scare'

Alternations show the productive nature of medial cluster agreement (21).

(21)

źa[b]a	'frog'	za[pk]a	'dim.'
ró[zg]a	'rod'	ró[štšk]a	'dim.'
wo[d]a	'water'	wó[tk]a	'vodka'
pro[ć]ić	'request,v'	pro[źb]a	noun
li[tš]yć	'count'	li[džb]a	'numeral'
wies[štš]yć	'prophesy'	wie[ždž]a	'prophecy'

Final clusters are voiceless, and the productive nature of word-final devoicing is demonstrated by alternations (22).

(22)
wo[d]a	'water'	wó[t]	gen.pl.
chel[b]a	'bread,gen.sg.'	chel[p]	nom.sg.
ka[ž]e	'he orders'	ka[š]	imper.
ró[zg]a	'rod'	ró[sk]	gen pl
wró[žb]a	'prophecy'	wró[šp]	gen pl
i[d]ẽ	'I go'	i[ćć]	inf
wio[d]ẽ	'I lead'	wie[ćć]	inf
kł a[d]ẽ	'I put'	kł a[ćć]	inf
gry[z]ẽ	'I bite'	gry[ćć]	inf
le[z]ẽ	'I scramble'	le[ćć]	inf

Although these clusters are more elaborate than those in Dutch or Catalan, the phenomenon of voicing assimilation and final devoicing has the same analysis: the combination of the Voice Constraint and spreading of [voice]. Word-final consonants are not pre-sonorant, so [voice] is unlicensed and deletes. In medial obstruent clusters, [voice] is only licensed in the last consonant before the vowel or prevocalic sonorant. [voice] will delink from all other consonants, and [voice] will spread to all other consonants in a cluster if the final obstruent is voiced.

Polish is unusual in consonant cluster possibilities; this is particularly true when sonorants are considered. Nearly all languages obey the sonority principle that requires sonorants to be closer to the nucleus than obstruents in a sequence. Polish allows clusters such as word-initial [rt] and word-final [tr] that violate this principle. Not surprisingly, this introduces some complexity into the analysis of voicing in clusters.

As expected given the form of the Voice Constraint, sonorants can combine with either voiced or voiceless consonants (23a) in initial clusters. More unexpected is the fact that there is voice agreement in clusters that ignores an intervening sonorant (23b) (I will argue that the devoicing of the sonorant is phonetic, not phonological).

(23)
a. [zn]ak   'sign'   [sn]op   'sheaf'
   [gr]ono   'cluster'   [kr]owa   'cow'
   [zv]ój   'coil'   [sf]ój   'one'sown'

b. [kr̩t]an 'larynx'   [grd]yka   'Adam's apple'
   mẽ[d]rek 'wiseacre'   mẽ[tr̩k]owa 'wisecrack, verb'

If [voice] is truly licensed before a sonorant consonant, as well as before a vowel, we would expect that initial clusters such as [grt] would be possible: [voice] in [g] would be licensed before [r], which is [+son]. (We would not expect the opposite, [krd], simply because Spreading would voice the initial [k].)

The Voice Constraint predicts that if the sonorants were syllabic, a sequence like [#gr.tV] would be possible, where the initial consonant directly precedes the peak of its syllable. But crucially in Polish, the entire sequence obstruent-sonorant-obstruent is a syllable onset. This means that the impossibility of clusters like [#grt] is ruled out by the Universal Sonority constraint, which does not allow a voiceless obstruent to intervene between a voiced obstruent and a syllable nucleus. This is an absolute universal that no language can violate; Polish obeys it, even though its syllable possibilities are unusual in other ways. Other syllabification facts that are referred to sonority are susceptible to language-particular variation, but this principle is not. Thus this cluster is ruled out by universal principles and is repaired by delinking, presumably the universal default repair strategy.

Sonorants in medial clusters are subject to the same analysis. In an example like m̃e[tr̩k]owa, the entire sequence is syllabified as an onset (Gussman ms., Bethin 1989). Thus the same principles will hold as in the word-initial cases in (23b): it is subject to Universal Sonority, which will forbid the sequence [drk] syllable-initially.

The type of onset in (23a) can also occur word-medially:

(24)
o.[gw]ada 'good manners'   o[kw]ada   'he covers'
pi.[ž]mo   'musk'   pi[sm]o   'writing'

The present theory requires the syllabification given for the examples in the first column, since syllable-final consonants cannot be voiced. This is also the syllabification proposed by Gussman and Bethin. Gussman and Bethin, in detailed discussions of Polish syllable structure, also propose that many segments in word-internal clusters remain unsyllabified until quite late, adjoining only to the word and not to any syllables. For example, Bethin gives the example *piosnka*, which she syllabifies as in (25):

(25)

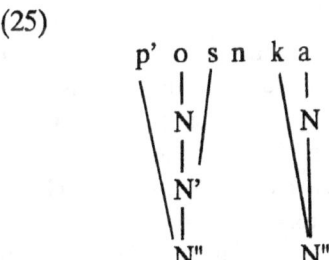

If this is correct, it will correctly predict that the [s] preceding [n] also cannot be licensed for [voice]; although it is an obstruent preceding a sonorant, this is not the syllable configuration required by the Voice Constraint. Gussman's analysis is somewhat different but also involves word-internal unsyllabified segments. The only aspect of Polish syllabification which is crucial to the Voice Constraint is that these consonants are *not* in onsets; there seems to be general agreement on this point, despite disagreement on the details.

The remaining complication regarding sonorants involves the word-final clusters with sonorants following obstruents. There is devoicing of sonorants between voiceless stops, and word-finally after voiceless stops (26a). Under the present theory, this devoicing must be phonetic, since sonorants cannot be phonologically marked for voicelessness. An unexpected fact under the present theory is that obstruents in final clusters devoice even when preceding a sonorant (26b), as if the sonorant were invisible for the purposes of counting the obstruent as word-final.

(26)
  a. ry[tm̩]   'rhythm'   [kr̥t]an   'larynx'
     cy[kl̩]   'cycle'
     fil[tr̩]   'filter'

  b. kadmu   'cadmium, gen. sg.'   ka[tm̩]   nom. sg.
     bo[br]a   'beaver, gen. sg.'   bó[pr̩]   nom. sg.
     żu[br]y   'bison, nom. pl.'   żu[pr̩]   nom. sg.
     boja[źń]i 'fear, gen. sg.'   boja[źn̩] nom. sg.

Many of the examples given here (from Gussman) are loans, but this does not appear to be of any significance, and not merely because these are loans from languages that do not allow such clusters. Bethin refers to a study of consonant clusters by Bargiełowna (1950); eliminating rare clusters and those appearing only in loans, this still leaves *-pr, -tr, -sm, -śń*. Thus word-final obstruent-sonorant clusters are a real possibility and must be accounted for. The difficulty is again that the expectation would be that [voice] could be licensed in the [t] in *ka[tm]*, since it precedes a sonorant. Again, the answer lies in details of the syllabification of Polish. Given the hypothesis mentioned above, that only a single sonorant can end a syllable in Polish, it is clear that some special mechanism is involved here. In a framework such as Bethin's, these consonants can only be adjoined to the word at a late stage; they cannot be syllabified by the usual procedures. If these segments are actually attached at the word level and not to a syllable node, they will not have the structure required by the Voice Constraint, which specifically mentions the syllable tier. Other analyses that differ in detail will also produce the same result; the crucial point is that these segments do not receive the normal syllabification, and thus will not conform to the Constraint, since the obstruent precedes the sonorant but is not tautosyllabic with it.

    Polish also has progressive assimilation in a few restricted cases. [ž] is derived from underlying [r] by palatalization. Its voicing is determined by the voicing of the preceding obstruent:

(27)
[gr]a 'game' [gž]e loc. sg.
[kr]a 'ice float' [kš]e loc. sg.
wia[tr]u 'wind, gen.sg.' wie[t-š]e loc. sg.
wie[t-š]ny 'windy'

A similar alternation exists with [v, f].

(28)
cerkie[vn]y 'Orthodox' cer[kf']i 'Orthodox church, gen. sg.'
bite[vn]y 'of the fight' bi[tf]a 'fight'

With [ž] the process is exceptionless, but according to Gussman, with [v] there is considerable variation depending on style and dialect; in some, voiceless obstruent-[v] is possible. Underlying sequences show the same variation as well:

(29)
[tf]ój, [tv]ój 'your'
[sv]oboda, [sf]oboda

I will discuss the [r] alternation, since it is more regular. The [v/f] alternation can be analyzed in the same way as the [ž/š] alternation, if [v] is underlyingly a sonorant (a not uncommon situation) and there is an rule of obstruentization as above, but which is optional.
   Since [r] is a sonorant, it has no [voice] specification underlyingly. If the obstruentization rule changes only [+son] to [-son], the result will be an obstruent with no [voice] specification.

(30)
                    /gre/
Obstruentization   gše
Surface form   gže

When the last obstruent in a cluster is voiceless, normally the whole cluster is voiceless. However, in these cases, and these cases only, voicing spreads to the right, to the former sonorant.

One possibility to explain these facts is that the rule of [voice] spread is not directional. Imagine that [voice] simply spreads to all adjacent legitimate bearers. Because of how the neutralization process works, all non-prevocalic [voice] will be unlicensed and will delink. Thus, the only possible targets for spread will be to the left, and the only possible place for [voice] to spread from will be the rightmost, prevocalic segment. The apparent directionality of [voice] spread would be an accident, then, and not a property of the rule.

This view of [voice] spread accounts for the Polish facts. It runs into difficulties in the case of languages that have only Spreading without Neutralization, such as Swedish and Ukranian (discussed below). The difference between these languages is that Polish obstruent clusters agree in voicing, and Swedish and Ukranian ones do not necessarily. Possibly in the first type of language, spreading is bidirectional, but not in the second, although it is not clear how the theory could capture this correlation. The evidence to test this is extremely difficult to come by; we would need a language without neutralization, with spreading, and that had an obstruentization process like the one in Polish. The Polish case is unusual in that an underlyingly licensed [voice] becomes unlicensed without changing its syllabic affiliation--the very syllabic affiliation that made it licensed in the first place. The result of the obstruentization process, if it were to remain a voiceless obstruent, would be a violation of the Universal Sonority constraint. [voice] can spread to the right to repair this violation; it is probably best to consider this a special case.

Some additional facts about Polish voicing spread between words and the behavior of sonorants will be discussed in chapter 4.

2.2.2 Neutralization only: German

German is a well-known case that is described as having syllable-final devoicing. This is shown in the following examples (some from Mascaro ms.). The (a) examples show consonants that are underlying voiced, and remain voiced if they are syllable-initial, for example when there is a vowel-initial suffix. The (b) examples show that the consonants become voiceless when syllable-final: either when they are word-final, or when a consonant suffix is added, whether voiced or voiceless:

(31)
    a. run[d]e   'round plu.'
       Run.[d]ung   'rounding, labialization'
    b. run[t]   'round sng.'
       Run[tb]au   'rotunda'
       Run[tv]orm   'roundworm'
       Run[tg]ang   'stroll'
       Run[t]gesang   'round (song)'
       Run[ts]äule   'cylinder'
       Run[ts]trickmachine   'circular knitting machine'

(32)
    a. lö[z]en   'to loosen, dissolve'
       Lö[z]ung   'solution'
       Lö[z]emittel   'solvent'
    b. lo[s]   'loose'
       lö[sb]ar   'solvable'
       Lö[sl]ich   'soluble'
       lö[st]   '(3rd per.sg.)'

(33)
    a. We[g]e   'way, dat.'
       We[ge]netz   'road network'
       We[g]elager   'highway robber'
    b. We[k]   'way, nom.'
       We[kš]necke   'slug (path + snail)'
       We[k]bereiter   'pioneer'
       We[km]arkierung   'road marker'
       We[kš]pur   'trace'

Note that in the example 'lo[st]' the entire coda is voiceless: [z] devoices before the ending [t].

German devoicing can be described as syllable-final. But the Voice Constraint gives the correct results without a specific rule of syllable-final delinking. German is a language that has the Voice Constraint: only onset consonants can bear [voice]. [voice] in any other position will violate the constraint, and the violation is repaired by delinking. Thus, the first consonant in a medial cluster, the final consonant in a word, and any consonant in a final cluster will become voiceless.

German shows that the Voice Constraint may hold only at a particular level in a language. Syllable-final consonants are not uniformly voiceless on the surface in German. (Data from Rubach 1990):

(34)
Handl+ung -> Han[d]lung, but hand+lich -> han[t]lich
similarly: *voiced*   *voiceless*
        Ordn+ung   Bild+nis
        ebn+en   Ergeb+nis
        Begegn+ung   Wag+nis
        eign+en   Zeug+nis
        nebl+ig   glaub+lich

The difference between the forms in the two columns is that in the forms in the first column, the stop is underlyingly syllable-initial. In other forms of these morphemes, this is true on the surface: the written form has a vowel, and the syllable is pronounced with a schwa or syllabic sonorant as syllable peak.

(35) handel+n, eben, eigen, Nebel

Thus it is possible to conclude that the forms in the first column have a vowel slot underlyingly. This vowel slot deletes when the vowel-initial suffixes are attached and the vowel is in an open syllable. Thus the derivation of "eignen":

(36)
    UF: eigVn+en
    devoicing: Does not apply: [g] is not syllable-final
    vowel deletion: eignen

There are no such alternate forms with vowels of the morphemes in the second column. Their underlying forms are roughly the same as their surface forms in syllabification, so the stops in question will be syllable-final, and will devoice. The difference between the forms in the two columns in (34), then, derives from the different syllable structures of the underlying forms.[4] The Voice Constraint is only active on an early level of syllabification in German. Such a stipulation would be necessary in any analysis since the items in the second column show that the description that syllable-final consonants are voiceless in German does not hold of surface form.

2.2.3 Spreading only: Swedish, Ukrainian

Swedish (Sigurd 1965) allows only the following medial stop clusters:

(37)   gd dg pt kt dk

(Fricatives are irrelevant--Swedish has only voiceless fricatives except for [v], which acts like a sonorant. There are some exceptions: *kd, tg*; but Sigurd is clear that these are marginal, occurring mostly in borrowings, such as *synekdoke*.) Although the combinations are few in number, the generalization is that only the following sequences are permitted:
   voiced-voiced   voiceless-voiceless   voiced-voiceless
Since voiced-voiceless clusters are permitted, and final consonants may be voiced, Swedish does not have the Voice Constraint. The combination that is missing is voiceless-voiced. This is to be expected if Swedish has the [voice] spread rule at the lexical level. (Voicing apparently works differently in some morphological alternations, but I have been unable to obtain enough data to attempt an analysis.)

The same situation holds in Ukrainian (Humesky 1980, Zilyns'kj 1979; again, the sources give no evidence for morphological alternations, but the facts seem clear for lexical clusters.) The only cases of devoicing before a voiceless consonant are in a prefix /z/, for which devoicing is fairly regular, and prefixes /bez, roz/, for which devoicing is less frequent. A special rule for these cases, combined with the fact that Ukrainian has [voice] spread, will account for these.

2.2.4 Final Exceptionality

Yiddish has assimilation in consonant clusters but allows voiced obstruents finally (Katz 1987).[5]

(38)
[šrayb]	'I write'	[red]	'I speak'
[vog]	'weight'	[ayz]	'ice'
[briv]	'letter'		
[vokšoi]	'scale'	[ayskastn]	'icebox'
[briftreger]	'mailman'		
[bak]	'cheek'	[bagbeyn]	'cheekbone'
[švitsn]	'sweat, v.'	[švidzbod]	'steambath'
[zis]	'sweet'	[zizvarg]	'candy products'
[kop]	'head'	[kobveytik]	'headache'

shrayb + st -> [šraypst]   'you (fam.) write'
red + st -> [retst]   'you (fam.) speak'

Yiddish must have the Voice Constraint and spreading, since it has voicing assimilation. But final voiced consonants are allowed, although such consonants cannot be licensed by the Voice Constraint.[6] Thus it must have the property of Final Exceptionality explained in the outline of the theory, above.

Serbo-Croatian (Hodge 1946) and Romanian (Agard 1950, Belchita 1967) are two more languages for which this analysis is required, at least for lexical consonant clusters (I have no relevant morphological information for these languages); medial clusters agree in voicing, and there is a final voiced/voiceless contrast. Hungarian is also a language of this type, with evidence from morphological alternations as well (Vago 1980, Kálmán 1972).

(39) Hungarian
kalap	'hat'	kala[bb]an	'in the hat'
kút	'well'	kú[db]an	'in the well'
ráb	'prisoner'	ra[pt]ól	'from the prisoner'
kád	'tub'	ká[tt]ól	'from the tub'

2.3 Predictions of possible theories

The following table shows all possible combinations of the mechanisms proposed, and the languages that exemplify them.

(40)

Voice Constraint (Neutralization)	Spread	Final Ex.	
x			German
x	x		Polish, Dutch, Catalan
x	x	x	Yiddish, Hungarian, Romanian, Serbo-Croatian
	x		Swedish, Ukrainian
x		x	(see below)

There are only 6 possibilities because Final Exceptionality is only meaningful in the presence of the Voice Constraint. The sixth possibility is a language that has none of these mechanisms, and so allows all possible combinations of voicing in obstruent clusters, such as English. (English does have some restrictions on clusters, but they apply only at level 1; this is discussed further in chapter 3. Additional examples mentioned by Cho (1990a) are Kannada and Tulu.)

Cases like Dutch are what would be expected in a theory of neutralization and spreading like the one I propose; one expects to find word-final devoicing whenever a language has assimilation in clusters, since such languages must have the Voice Constraint. Assimilation in internal clusters does not always correlate with final devoicing, however. Dutch, Catalan, and Polish have assimilation and final devoicing; Yiddish, Serbo-Croatian, Hungarian and Romanian have assimilation and no final devoicing. These are the languages that, under the present analysis, have Final Exceptionality. Thus the latter languages are somewhat more complex in their analysis, and we should consider whether this is correct. The question is, which is the normal case, and which is the case that should be handled with additional theoretical machinery?

Many possible theories would predict the same markedness relations. For instance if neutralization were stated as syllable-final, something like final extrametricality would still be needed to prevent neutralization in cases like Yiddish, since word-final consonants are also syllable-final. So in such a theory it would also be the case that Yiddish would be exceptional, and Dutch would be normal. (The problems with a theory of syllable-final neutralization will be discussed later.)

Instead, the processes of internal neutralization and word-final devoicing could be separated entirely, even in a theory where assimilation consisted of neutralization and spreading. There could be preobstruent neutralization, which would apply in clusters; spreading; and a separate rule of word-final neutralization.

However, such a theory makes incorrect predictions about possible languages. It accounts for Yiddish and Dutch, but it also predicts that a language could have word-final devoicing, but no neutralization in clusters. I have found no languages of this type. Final devoicing always cooccurs with either cluster assimilation (as in Dutch) or word-internal 'syllable-final' devoicing (as in German), both of which are evidence of the Voice Constraint.

The present theory accounts for this, using the well-known insight that the edges of words can be exceptional in the phonology of a language. The Voice Constraint predicts that there will be devoicing or assimilation internally, and word-final devoicing. But because word edges can be exceptional, the latter may not occur. The nonoccurring case, word-final devoicing and no voicing effects in internal clusters, could not be analyzed by this theory.

Word-final delinking as a separate rule would also incorrectly predict that word-initial delinking is possible. Kaye (1979) suggest that Lac Simon Algonquian has word-initial devoicing, but this analysis is convincingly refuted by Iverson (1983).

A slight embarrassment to the present theory is the missing case: a language with word-internal 'syllable-final' devoicing and final voiced consonants. This would be a language like German but with a final voicing contrast. All of the languages that I use to demonstrate word-internal neutralization are languages with voicing agreement: they have neutralization, but they also have spreading.[7] I would argue that this missing case is merely a consequence of the fact that [voice] has an overwhelming tendency to spread in clusters, making the required evidence hard to come by. But as I will show later, the other laryngeal features, glottalization and aspiration, show the same neutralization behavior as voicing: constraints of the same form as the Voice Constraint occur for glottalization, aspiration, and the Laryngeal Node as a whole. While spreading of [voice] is quite common, spreading of the other laryngeal features is much less common. Thus, evidence of word-internal neutralization without word-final neutralization is much easier to come by: Tojolabal is such a case, for glottalization.

2.3.1 Other theories of voicing assimilation

Analyses of voicing assimilation as neutralization and spreading have been proposed recently by Mascaro (ms.), and by Gussman (ms.) and Bethin (1989) for Polish.[8] All of these have in common the fact that obstruents unmarked for [voice] are said to have the value [-voice] filled in at a later stage, although all could probably be easily modified to accommodate a privative [voice] feature-- simply leaving unmarked consonants unmarked instead of filling in a default [-voice]. Thus the real question is is not about [-voice] but about whether the theories of neutralization proposed are coherent. Mascaro does not address the question of precisely what the domain of neutralization is. Gussman deletes [voice] in all syllabically unlicensed consonants. This theory requires some very specific notions about Polish syllable structure that will not extend to other languages in any obvious way. Bethin's theory is most similar to the present theory, as the proposes that [voice] is only licensed in onsets. Because the constraint refers to onsets, she requires a more elaborate model of syllable structure not required by the present theory. The work of Rubach and Booij (1990) on voice assimilation in Polish is discussed in Chapter 4.

Cho (1990a,b) also proposes that [voice] can be a privative feature if voicing assimilation is analyzed as neutralization and spreading. In this theory, neutralization may be coda-delinking, cluster delinking, or word-final delinking. I will now turn to the problems encountered by these other theories of the domain of neutralization.

2.3.1.1 Syllable-final neutralization. Neutralization is commonly referred to as syllable-final. A theory of syllable-final neutralization encounters serious problems with a language like Polish for two reasons. First of all, many analyses of Polish (e.g. Bethin 1989, Gussman ms.) argue that only sonorants are allowed in codas. In these analyses medial obstruent sequences are either in the onset or in some cases unsyllabified till late in the derivation, when they are attached at some other level of structure, yet they do devoice. Since these consonant sequences are not syllable-final, we cannot account for agreement with a rule of syllable-final neutralization.

The second problem for syllable-final delinking in Polish is the case of these complex onsets. This is a problem both medially and initially if the above analyses of syllable structure are correct, but let us consider the more obvious case of the word-initial onsets. In cases where the onset is voiced, this can be achieved by spreading. But in cases where the onset is voiceless, this cannot be achieved by syllable-final neutralization, since onset consonants are not syllable-final.[9]

This objection could be answered by the use of the Universal Sonority condition: The sequence voiced-voiceless-nucleus is universally prohibited. Presuming that such a violation is universally repaired by delinking, the facts about Polish onsets can be covered. An onset like *#pz* will become *#bz* because of the voice spread rule; an onset like *#bs* is prohibited by Greenberg's universal and becomes *#ps* by delinking.

This theory would run into difficulty in the case of the obstruentization of [r -> ž]; recall that this case gave evidence for needing spread to the right in some cases like *#bs*. In order to analyze agreement of voicelessness in onsets as a result of Universal Sonority and delinking, an alternative analysis of agreement in the obstruentization cases would be needed.

Another objection to syllable-final neutralization is that it must actually be stated as coda neutralization, and an attempt to formalize coda neutralization runs into difficulties. In languages with word-final devoicing, all word-final obstruent clusters are voiceless; a cluster like *dz#* surfaces as *ts#*. Syllable-final delinking would only give *ds#*, which is incorrect. Thus the rule must actually delink [voice] from codas. Many well-supported treatments of syllable structure do not include a coda constituent (see McCarthy and Prince (forthcoming and references therein), and if these theories are correct a rule of coda-delinking cannot be the correct analysis. But even in a theory with a coda constituent, a problem with this is the possibility that not all word-final consonants in a cluster are part of the coda. For instance, word-final consonant clusters in German are uniformly voiceless. But German syllable structure, like English, allows additional word-final coronals as part of a syllable appendix. Halle and Vergnaud (1980) propose the structure in (41):

(41)
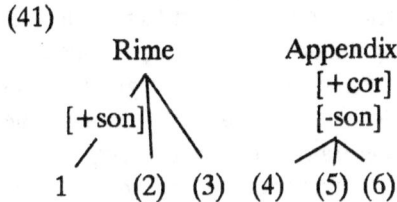

This structure accounts for the fact that while both *uns* and *eins* are well formed, *Kampf* is well-formed and **keimpf* is not. In the latter, the affricate [pf] would have to be in the appendix, since the diphthong and [m] are filling positions 1, 2, and 3. Thus the syllable is ill-formed, since [pf] is not a coronal and so cannot be part of the appendix. It follows, then, that in a word like *Feind*, the final consonant is not in the coda, but in the appendix. Nevertheless it does devoice.

Another argument against coda-delinking is that it predicts that onset-delinking is also possible: if we can write a rule that says "Delink at right edge" we would expect that "left edge" would also be an option. Such a process is unattested.

Since the issue of predictions about constituent edges has been brought up, the theory I propose must also be examined in light of these issues. Coda-delinking predicts onset-delinking, and word-final delinking predicts word-initial delinking; these are unattested processes, and the fact that these theories predict unattested processes is an argument against them. Are there similar options with the Voice Constraint and final exceptionality; do these mechanisms predict other options for edges or directionality? If coda delinking predicts onset delinking, can we apply this argument to the present theory?

This would mean arguing that "[voice] is licensed only before [+son] in the same syllable" predicts "[voice] only after [+son] in the same syllable "or for that matter, "[voice] only before obstruent in the same syllable" or "[+son] in a different syllable." I would argue that these extensions are invalid. It should be correct that using the primitive "word-edge" combined with the option "right", you predict the primitive can combine with the option "left." But the constraint that I propose is not composed of such options. This constraint is trying to capture an insight that is not composed of our current theoretical primitives, which combine with options about directionality and edges. Its form arises from deeper principles that are not subject to this variation. The principles have something to do with [voice] in obstruents only being able to appear before a more sonorous segment (vowel or sonorant), or, for a more radical proposal, before a segment that is also voiced (although sonorant and vowel voicing, which is not distinctive, would not be underlying in most current frameworks, so the insight could not be expressed in this way.) Although I have argued that 'release' as currently understood cannot be used to explain the phonology of voicing, the insight that the theory is trying to capture is similar in a crucial way: the transition from consonant to vowel (or to other sonorous segment) has special properties. There is something important about this particular transition, in a way that does not admit of using the left/right distinction to cross-classify it, the way the left/right distinction can cross-classify word edges or sonority (towards the nucleus/away from the nucleus). The transition from vowel to consonant is not comparable; directionality is not an option, because it is the particular direction that is crucial and that has special properties.

Another question about directionality for the present theory has to do with final exceptionality. I argued earlier that word-final delinking would predict word-initial delinking, which does not occur. Likewise, if Final Exceptionality is a particular type of extrametricality, we expect that Initial Exceptionality would occur: that initial consonants could be invisible to the constraint. Initial extrametricality is less common than final extrametricality, and we might expect the same relation to hold. But consider what would happen when initial exceptionality did occur. If initial consonants are invisible to the constraint, however, all this means is that word-initial voiced consonants will be allowed in languages that have the Voice Constraint. The Voice Constraint licenses those consonants anyway; a language with the constraint and Initial Exceptionality would look exactly the same as a language with only the constraint, as far as single initial consonants.

In clusters, Initial Exceptionality would allow a sequence like #$_{em}$(z)t. However, this would be ruled out by the Universal Sonority constraint that prohibits the sequence voiced-voiceless-nucleus. This is a universal constraint, not a language-particular fact like the Voice Constraint, which is presumably why it is unaffected by the extrametrical status of the consonant--although languages can make certain choices about their sonority hierarchies, they cannot violate universal principles, for example they cannot make consonants more sonorous than vowels.

Thus, initial clusters would also look the same in both languages, the one with the constraint and initial exceptionality, and the one with only the constraint. Since there can be no evidence for the more complex analysis--with Initial Exceptionality--and the languages generated would look identical, presumably the language learner will always choose the grammar that does not have Initial Exceptionality. Thus, the option of Initial Exceptionality may exist, and makes no incorrect predictions about possible languages; however, it seems unlikely that such an analysis would remain in a grammar for very long.

2.3.1.2 Preobstruent or cluster neutralization. Syllable-final delinking runs into its most serious empirical difficulties in the analysis of a language like Polish, where all clusters agree in voicing regardless of syllable structure. Polish could be analyzed by a rule that delinks [voice] before another obstruent. This preobstruent neutralization cannot by itself account for all the facts. It can account for Polish onsets, for instance, but cannot account for final devoicing, since final consonants are not before an obstruent. Thus, we would need a combined theory in which pre-obstruent and syllable-final neutralization were both possible options. This is roughly the theory of Cho (1990a,b), where her cluster-delinking is equivalent to preobstruent neutralization, so I will evaluate the version of this theory that Cho presents.

Cho's theory requires three types of delinking: coda-delinking, cluster-delinking, and word-final delinking. Coda-delinking is used to account for languages like German and Dutch. Cluster-delinking accounts for a language such as Serbo-

Croatian, where there is neutralization in clusters but no word-final devoicing. But cluster-delinking must also be used to account for Polish (Cho uses the example of Russian), yet this will not account for the fact that the language has devoicing of final consonants. Thus, a separate rule of word-final delinking is added to the analysis to account for this. As I have already discussed in section 2.3.1, this makes the incorrect predictions, since word-final neutralization never occurs without evidence of word-internal neutralization. Cho claims to predict six types of languages with the interaction of the two spreading and neutralization parameters:

		Spreading	
		+	−
Devoicing:	coda	Dutch	German
	cluster	Serbo-Croatian	Kirghiz
	none	Ukrainian	Kannada

In fact, the theory predicts more types of languages than this if we factor in the separate word-final rule. Crucially, it predicts that languages could have only word-final delinking, without any other kind of neutralization. This would be a language that had word-final devoicing, but did not have either word-internal syllable-final neutralization or voicing assimilation. This type of language appears not to exist.

In addition, there does not seem to be any reason why the different types of neutralization combine as they do in this theory. A language can have cluster-delinking and word-final delinking, so why does a language never have both coda-delinking and cluster-delinking? The reason for this is that this type of delinking is claimed to be a parameter, so that only one choice is made, while word-final delinking is a separate rule, not an option of a the parameter. There is no principled reason for this distinction; it is a stipulation that is necessary to account for the facts in this system.

2.3.2 Conclusions

The analyses in this chapter show that the Voice Constraint, a positive constraint on the licensing of a feature, can account for voicing assimilation and neutralization. The important difference between the alternative theories I have outlined and the theory I propose is that these alternative theories specify where voice is disallowed, rather than where voice is allowed. Ito (1986) shows that positive and negative constraints are formally equivalent. However, though you can give a formal statement of any negative constraint as a positive constraint (and vice versa), other aspects of phonological theory may determine the correct statement. For instance, Ito (1986, p 88) gives a preliminary formulation of the coda constraint in Lardil as a negative constraint forbidding [-cor]. She reformulates this as a positive constraint to account for additional data, and it also is clear that this would have to be a positive constraint only because [cor] is a privative feature. Thus both the data and the theory determine that this constraint can only be stated positively. In the case of the Voice Constraint, the previous two sections show that theories that attempt to account for these facts by way of a negative constraint run into difficulties; thus, in order to account for all the relevant facts and make the correct predictions, a positive constraint is necessary.

2.4 Other possible counterevidence

There are two other phenomena that are a potential problem for the theory of privative voicing. Dahl's Law in Bantu, and to a lesser extent Thurneysen's Law in Gothic, have been analyzed as dissimilation of voicelessness. If dissimilations are effects of the OCP, this is a problem for the privative voicing theory: we cannot rule out adjacent [-voice] if [-voice] does not exist. I will show that this phenomenon can be analyzed in a way that is consistent with privative voicing. Another question is that of the existence of voiceless sonorants. The issue is that there is evidence that plain voiced sonorants are unmarked for [voice]. If this is the case, then voiceless sonorants cannot be sonorants without laryngeal features. In chapter 4 I will argue that voiceless sonorants should be analyzed as aspirated, the solution proposed by Mester and Ito (1989).

2.4.1 Dissimilation of [-voice]

Dahl's Law in Bantu is a historical process, but one that also exists synchronically in Kikuyu (Armstrong 1967, Davy and Nurse 1982, Barlow 1960) and other related languages. The traditional description says that k-initial prefixes become voiced (they will surface as [ɣ]) when the initial consonant of the following syllable is voiceless. I will first review some relevant facts about Kikuyu phonology.

(42) Kikuyu phonemes:

Bilabial	Dental	Alveolar	Alv-pal	Palatal	Velar	Glottal
		t			k	
			c			
mb		nd	nj		ng	
ß	ð	r			ɣ	
m		n		ñ	ŋ	
w				y		h

[ð] is the traditional transcription of the dental sound, but it behaves in all ways as voiceless. It does not pattern with the voiced fricatives in hardening, and it patterns with the voiceless stops in Dahl's Law. This leads to the conclusion that it is underlyingly voiceless (Davy and Nurse assume this also). However, I will continue to use the traditional transcription. Tone will be omitted throughout. The relevant phonological processes of the language are as follows:

Postnasal hardening affects [ß, r, ɣ], which become stops after a nasal. [t,c,k] become voiced after a nasal by another rule. Nasals delete before [ð,h], and other nasals. Presumably there is no hardening of [ð] because, assuming it is the voiceless dental stop, it has no prenasalized voiced counterpart. I assume the analysis of these facts given in Lombardi (1990b), which derives the results from a requirement that the nasal must share place with a following [-cont]. The following examples all are adjectives used with Nasal Group nouns. (I omit examples of vowel-initial stems that show the operation of some additional irrelevant rules of long-distance dissimilation of nasals and prenasals.)

(43)
Postnasal hardening:

ngwace mbuðu	'rotten potatoes'	o-ßudu	'rotteness'
nguuo ndoi	'fierce hippo'	o-roi	'fierceness'
ñoombo ngootaru	'idle mule'	o-ɣoota	'idleness'

Postnasal voicing:

ñoomba ndɔɔngu	'wealthy house'	o-tɔɔngu	'wealth'
ñɔni ngƐnu	'happy birds'	o-kƐnu	'happiness'
njera njƐkƐ	'narrow road'	o-cƐkƐ	'narrowness'

Deletion of nasal:

nguuo ne nɔru	'hippo is fat'	o-nɔru	'fatness'
njata ðƐru	'bright star'	o-ðƐru	'brightness'
ñama hɔrɔ	'cold meat'	o-hɔrɔ	'coldness, softness'

Before vowels: nasal prefix *nj*

| ŋɔɔmbƐ njiro | 'black cow' | o-iro | 'blackness' |
| nguuo njee | 'fierce hippo' | wee | 'fierceness' |

In the Dahl's Law cases, certain prefixes are k-initial in some situations and ɣ-initial in others. The prefix will begin with [ɣ] when the next syllable begins with [ð, t, c, k], (recall that ð is underlyingly voiceless), and will begin with [k] everywhere else-- including when the next syllable begins with a vowel or [h]. [h] is voiced post-vocalically according to Davy and Nurse, which is consistent with its patterning with the voiced sounds here. In fact Davy and Nurse seem to consider that the basic phoneme is voiced. They state that /ß, ɦ/ have phrase initial voiceless variants, but in the relevant environment, which is postvocalic, are always voiced.

(44)

ko-ruɣa	'to cook'	ɣo-tƐŋƐra	'to run'
ko-oria	'to ask' (koo.ria)	ɣo-ciimba	'to hoe'
ko-mƐña	'to know'	ɣo-ðƐka	'to laugh'
ko-fiɔta	'to be able'	ɣo-koora	'to root out'
ko-niina	'to finish'		

The following examples show that it is the immediately following syllable that is crucial, and also show the effect of vowel-initial syllables. For example, observe the second morpheme in these words: it is [kaa] when followed by a vowel-initial syllable, even though the next consonant in the word is [k]; it is [ɣaa] when immediately followed by a [k]-initial syllable.

(45)
a. ndo.kaa.Ɛ.kwa.nde.ka 'Don't on any account write'
ndo.kaa.Ɛ.ko.hƐƐ.a.na 'Don't on any account give away'
ndo.ɣaa.ke.Ɛ.ko.ɣo.ra 'Now whatever you do, don't buy'
ndo.ɣaa.ke.Ɛ.ko.rea 'Now whatever you do, don't eat'
(Armstrong)
b. [a.ke.o.ña] varies with [a.ɣeo.ki.ña]
'and he trod on it' (Davy and Nurse)

There are no invariant /g/ or /ɣ/ initial suffixes in Kikuyu with which the /k/-initial suffixes contrast, nor are there any non-alternating /k/-initial suffixes.

Crucial to the correct analysis of this process is the behavior of words with multiple velar prefixes. A fair amount of attention has been paid to the case where there is a string of velar-initial suffixes, since this has had considerable interest for the question of rule application (Davy and Nurse 1982, Pulleyblank 1986). Assuming the traditional analysis that these are underlyingly voiceless prefixes that become [+voice] as a result of dissimilation, the problematic cases are those such as the following:

(46) ke-ke-ke-θok-a -> [ɣeɣeɣeθoka]

Assuming cyclic derivation, an alternating [k..ɣ] pattern is expected, but this is not what happens.

First of all, prefixes do condition the rule: a prefix dissimilates with a following prefix. This appears to be true of velar prefixes as well, in sequences of no more than two.

(47)
  a. ndo-ɣaa-ke-ɛ-ko-niina
     ndo-kaa-na-ɛ-ko-niina   (Armstrong)
  b. ka-mu-ndu   'small person'
     mu-ndu   'person'
     ka-mu-ti   'small stick'
     ɣa-ti   'tiny stick'
     ka-ru-ku   'small piece of firewood'
     ɣa-ku   'fragment of firewood' (Barlow[10])
  c. ɣa-ta-kaa-roma   'the small thing
                           that will not bite'
     ɣa-ta-ɣaa-ko-roma 'the small thing that will not
                           bite you' (Davy and Nurse p164)

In all of these examples the velar prefix disagrees in voicing with the initial of the next syllable, even if the next syllable is also a prefix.

    Consider next strings of more than two velar prefixes. In these strings, the last velar prefix (marked * in the examples) disagrees in voicing with the first sound of the root. But all of the other prefixes appear in the voiced form, despite the fact that normally prefixes do dissimilate (those that would be expected to devoice are marked 'k'):

(48)
  a-ɣaa-ɣii-kia a-ɣe-ɣwee-ta
   k   *   k   *

  ɣa-ɣa-ko-roma
   k   *   (Davy and Nurse)

  u-ɣi-ɣa-kinya i-ɣi-ka-mera
   k *   *

  ɣi-ɣa-thii
   k *   (Barlow)

In fact, strings of velar prefixes, whether two or more than two, behave exactly the same way. The last in any string of velar prefixes devoices next to a voiced-initial syllable (recall that vowels count as such); any prefix other than the last remains unchanged.

(49)
two prefixes:
ndo-ɣaa-ke-ɛ-ko-niina
        *

ɣa-ta-ɣaa-ko-roma
     *

three prefixes:
    ɣa-ɣa-ko-roma
       *

This appears to be an OCP effect between the last prefix and the initial of the root. But since there is no OCP effect between prefixes, this is evidence that some kind of multiple linking is crucial to the analysis of this process.

Assume that the velar prefixes are underlying voiceless, which means they are without laryngeal features. A rule is needed that voices velar prefixes (50a). In the case of a word with a single prefix, this rule will fill in [voice] on the prefix, except when the initial of the root is voiced. The latter case would result in an OCP violation, so the rule is blocked (McCarthy 1986).

Strings of velar prefixes involve this voice default rule and a rule of spreading (50b). The rule that voices velar prefixes fills in [voice], linking it to the leftmost velar prefix; the spreading rule spreads [voice] to the right. [voice] is linked to the sound on the left edge of the syllable and spreads to succeeding left edges. However, spreading stops if it would cause an OCP violation (Myers 1987).[11]

(50)
a. ∅ -> [voice] / $_\sigma$[. Root
　　　　　　　　　|
　　　　　　　[dorsal]
　　　　　　　[-nasal]

b. Spread [voice] rightwards

Vowel-initial syllables cause the OCP effect because, being the first sound in their syllable, they are on the left edge, and are voiced. This brings us to the question of the status of voicing in sounds other than obstruents. Sonorants and vowels are generally assumed to be underspecified for [voice] since they do not contrast in this feature; yet voicing in these sounds does condition the OCP effect for Dahl's Law. [voice] also appears to spread from sonorants to obstruents in the rule of postnasal voicing; one could try to take the position that sonorants and vowels are simply not underspecified for [voice] in this language, since its phonology provides direct counterevidence for this assumption.

However, recall that what is relevant to the rule is surface syllabification, with varying effects in fast speech (example (45b) above). And if /h/ is underlyingly voiceless and [ɦ] is an allophone (the more common situation cross-linguistically), this is another case that makes it clear that a surface rather than underlying representation is what this rule affects, since /h/ patterns with voiced sounds.

Thus there is no counterevidence here to the claim that sonorants are underlyingly underspecified for [voice], since this rule affects a surface representation, presumably one in which redundant values have already been filled in. All sounds that are actually phonetically voiced--vowels, sonorants, and allophones of voiceless sounds--condition the OCP effect when they are on the left edge of the syllable. [ð] is also not a problem, since not even its allophones appear to be truly voiced. Davy and Nurse say that it is "voiceless lenis" but "in all contexts essentially *voiceless*, differing in this respect quite markedly from the voiced [ð] of our Meru informants, in whose speech the segment fails to condition [this process]."

The derivation, then, is as follows:

(51)
Underlying representation:

ka - ka - ko - roma

Fill in of [voice] in underspecified sounds:

ka - ka - ko - roma
         |
      [voice]

Voice fill-in and spread till OCP violation:

ɣa - ɣa - ko - roma

root (with association lines to voice tiers)

voice   voice

A derivation in which the conditioning sound was an obstruent would be essentially identical, except that the [voice] of that sound would be underlying.

A remaining point of the analysis is this: I have shown that the OCP-effect delinking must take place after redundant values of [voice] are filled in, since it is conditioned by syllable-initial sonorants and vowels, as well as obstruents. This means that [voice] must also be filled in on all the syllable-internal vowels as well, at this point. But these syllable-internal vowels do not count for the OCP effect; only the left edges of syllables are visible to the rule. Although I have no real explanation of this peculiar property, any formulation of the rule in any framework will have to deal with this fact.[12]

Synchronic versions of Dahl's Law differ in different Bantu languages but can be similarly analyzed as insertion of [voice]. In Kinyarwanda (Kimenyi 1979) both /t/ and /k/ -initial prefixes (there is no /p/) become voiced when attached to a voiceless-initial stem; in this language there is no spreading and the rule does not apply between prefixes, but only to the prefix closest to the stem:

(52)
   a. /tu-ta-ki-kuunda-a/ tutagukuunda 'if we don't like you'
   b. /tu-ki-ßon-a/   tukißona   'we see it'

Another interesting case is Kuria (Odden 1987, Odden p.c.). Kuria has both /g/ and /k/-initial prefixes. In Kikuyu, it could be argued that the velar prefixes ought to be underlying voiceless due to underspecification: since there are no contrasting /g/-initial prefixes, the minimally redundant underlying representation of the prefixes is unspecified for [voice]. But it turns out that this is not crucial: Kuria, with both voiced and voiceless velar prefixes, also has a rule filling in [voice] on the voiceless prefixes when the following syllable begins with a voiceless consonant. There is no spreading, but the rule is not restricted to the prefix closest to the stem as in Kinyarwanda; it reapplies, resulting in an alternating pattern (53a). The voiced prefixes are unaffected both by the rule, since they are already voiced (53b), and interestingly, by the OCP effect: underlying voiced segments do not dissimilate, but remain voiced (53c).

(53)
   a.
   oko-karaanga -> ogo-karaanga   'to fry'
   oko-ko-karaanga -> oko-go-karaanga   'to fry you'
   oko-ke-ko-karaangera -> ogo-ke-go-karaangera
                                   'to fry it for you'

   oko-ko-romera -> ogo-ko-romera   'to bite for you'
   oko-ke-ko-romera -> oko-ge-ko-romera   'to bite it for you'
   oko-ko-ke-gɛsɛra -> oko-go-ke-gɛsɛera   'to harvest it for you'

b.
oko-go-karaanga -> oko-go-karaanga
oko-go-romera -> oko-go-romera

c.
ge-gɛsa   'to harvest'
oko-go-ge-geɛsɛra   'to harvest it for it'

The evidence from these two languages also suggests a possible modification of the analysis of Kikuyu. The Kikuyu rule formulated above links [voice] to the leftmost velar and spreads it to the right until there is an OCP violation. In these languages, however, the voice fill-in rule must link to the *rightmost* possible consonant--the closest consonant to the stem that will not result in the OCP violation. [13] To make Kikuyu more consistent with these related languages, it could simply have the same voice fill-in rule as these languages and spreading to the left instead of the right.

Another possible case of voicing dissimilation is Thurneysen's Law in Gothic. In certain suffixes, under certain stress conditions, a fricative in a suffix is voiced if the preceding consonant in the word is voiceless, and voiceless if the preceding consonant is voiced. It is not clear whether this is a synchronic or only a diachronic process. Chomsky and Halle (1968) analyze this as a case of 'polarity dissimilation', a rule formulation requiring Greek letter variables that would need [-voice] to exist as a feature marking, but more modern analyses have discarded this formulation of the law. Flickinger (1981) argues that Thurneysen's law does not in fact exist, and that all of the examples used as evidence for it are the result of Verner's Law. Other sources (Collinge 1985, Voyles 1981) retain the law, stating it as a process of voicing an underlyingly voiceless fricative. With such a formulation, an analysis like that given above for Kikuyu is possible: the rule fills in [voice] except where an OCP violation with the preceding consonant would be created; in such a case, the fill-in of [voice] is blocked.

Notes

1. In Ito (1986) positive constraints are formulated as if-then statements; the Voice Constraint would be "If [voice], then the configuration in (1)". Goldsmith (1990) also develops a theory based upon certain syllable positions acting as licensers of autosegmental material. Positive and negative constraints are also explicitly discussed by Archangeli and Pulleyblank (1986).

2. This is only true of [l], not other liquids: e.g., [pédrə]. It is only true of labials: [síklə] 'cycle', [síglə] 'acronym'. Mascaró (1976) states that he knows of only these exceptions to the generalization: [bíblia, bíblik], and [rəpúblika] is in free variation with [rəpúplika].

Voicing also appears to assimilate from a sonorant in an onset to a preceding syllable-final obstruent, but only across certain types of boundaries. It does not occur in the examples given here, and the proposed syllabification seems to be the only way to account for these alternations; the examples that do show this phenomenon that are given in Mascaró and Wheeler (1979) are all across word boundaries or prefix boundaries. Voicing assimilation between words which involves sonorants is addressed in chapter 4.

3. Gussman transcribes the affricates as digraphs. Although Polish can contrast affricates with stop-fricative sequences, I have retained his transcriptions with the following typographical variants:

prepalatal	alveolar	palatoalveolar
ś, ź	s, z	š, ž

Polish vowels with nasal hooks are rendered herein with a tilde. Transcriptions with the hyphen ([t-š, d-ž]) are intended by Gussman to indicate that this is a sequence of stop and fricative, contrasting with the digraphs that are the affricates.

4. There is a considerable literature on the question of whether vowel-zero alternations in German should be analyzed by deletion or insertion of vowels. As indicated in the text, the neutralization facts require a deletion analysis. For more arguments for this type

of analysis see for example Strauss (1982), and for the opposing viewpoint, Giegerich (1985).

Rubach (1990) argues that German devoicing interacts with morpheme boundaries, on the basis of the data in (34). However, he gives no justification for his choice of vowelless underlying forms in the first column.

5. The examples from Katz (1987) are mostly compounds. The phonology of compounds can have different phonology from the rest of a language, but these facts were checked with native speakers using other morphology, and they are correct. For example, [aiz] 'ice' plus the suffix [keit] '-ness' yields a nonsense word that is pronounced [aiskeit].

Thanks to Molly Diesing for assistance with the German and Yiddish data.

6. Another solution would be to propose underlying final vowels for voiced-final words in the languages discussed in this section. This is the historical development in Yiddish and in some varieties of German, but I do not know of any evidence for this as the synchronic situation in the languages discussed in this section. If it could be shown to be true for all the languages of this type, the Voice Constraint would be all that was needed to account for the facts; final consonant exceptionality could be eliminated from the theory. Note, however, that it would also have to be true for the unrelated languages discussed in chapter 3 that have Final Exceptionality that affects the distribution of other laryngeal features. Perhaps a more useful line of inquiry would be to note that this is a case where word-final consonants are acting like onsets (see McCarthy and Prince forthcoming).

7. Cho (1990a,b) claims that Kirghiz is a case of this type. However, the sources on Kirghiz make it quite clear that this interpretation of the data (following Keating 1984) is incorrect. The voiced stops are described (Hebert and Poppe 1963) as "voiceless lenis" "medially adjacent to another stop", and voiced elsewhere. Cho apparently uses this description to transcribe /abdan/ (p. 29) as *apdan*. But the description says *adjacent*, not "before". Another source, Wurm (1949), transcribes the same example very clearly as *aBDan*, the capital letters being his

The Feature [voice] and Voicing Assimilation

transcription for the "voiceless mediae." It also seems quite clear the this is not a case of neutralization, but simply a slightly different realization of the voiced stops in this context, since Wurm is so careful to transcribe these differently from the phonemic voiceless stops. Although the present theory also predicts a case of this type, it seems fairly clear that Kirghiz is not it. In chapter 3 I show that Tojolabal shows this predicted pattern of laryngeal neutralization with its glottalized consonants.

8. As I was completing this work I received a revised version of Bethin (1989), in which the analysis of Polish voicing assimilation is more similar to the one I develop here, in that [voice] is taken to be a privative feature.

9. Recall that if Gussman and Bethin are correct about Polish syllable structure, there are no syllable-final obstruents until late in the phonology. Getting onset clusters to agree, then, is nearly the whole question of Polish; the only work done by syllable-final delinking would be to devoice word-final consonants.

Note that for a case like Yiddish, the syllable-final theory would also need the same Final Exceptionality mechanism as the theory I am proposing, as well as relying crucially on the Universal Sonority condition. Thus we cannot argue for one theory over the other on the basis of some raw number of theoretical devices needed, since they do not differ in this respect.

10. Barlow transcribes the voiced velar as [g], which I have changed to γ for consistency. However, Barlow's vowel transcriptions are different from the others, and I have preserved the vowel transcriptions of the various sources.

11. This is essentially identical to Myers' (1987) analysis of the spreading of high tone in Shona. Also, the idea that a fill-in rule is involved was suggested by a reviewer of Pulleyblank's squib, noted in his footnote 4.

It may also be possible to assume that the default rule fills in [voice] on the prefixes and then there is fusion (see Myers 1987, for example on Southern Karanga) but it is easier to understand the OCP effect if the analysis is stated as involving spreading.

Additional evidence that the OCP is active on [voice] in Kikuyu comes from the fact that there may also be a morpheme structure constraint prohibiting two [voice] in a word (or root?). Pulleyblank says that there is such a constraint, but does not give the source of this information. Davy and Nurse say that the process has affected stems diachronically, which would indicate that a morpheme structure constraint exists synchronically. A cursory examination of a Kikuyu dictionary revealed no counterexamples to the claim.

12. The traditional analysis of this as [-voice] dissimilation has no advantage in this respect, since vowel-initial syllables still interrupt dissimilation--it would still need to explain why there is no dissimilation between the voiceless sounds in a sequence like [...kaa.ɛ.ko....] (from example (45a)). In fact, an autosegmental analysis assuming [-voice] dissimilation is difficult to construct. The crucial forms to explain are those with more than one velar prefix, which clearly exhibit multiple-linking behavior, such as those repeated here:

a. ka-kaa-kwee-ta -> ga-ga-gwee-ta
b. ki-ka-thii -> gi-ga-thii
c. ka-ka-ko-roma -> ga-ga-ko-roma
d. ki-ka-mera -> gi-ka-mera

In (a) and (b), all prefixes become voiced before a voiceless consonant. This is easily captured autosegmentally, assuming multiple linking:

```
         k k k   t
          \|/    |
         -voice -voice
dissim:    |
           ↓
         +voice
```

Assuming the same multiple linking makes it difficult to analyze (c) and (d), however. The first step of the derivation would need to be: In a sequence of linked [-voice], the last one delinks:

The Feature [voice] and Voicing Assimilation   75

```
k k k r        k    k   k
 \|/      ->    \/     |
  |            [-voice] [-voice]
[-voice]
```

This creates an OCP violation, and then dissimilation takes place between the [-voice] of the prefixes. Although once you have done the first step, dissimilation is the same as above, there seems to be no motivation for the first step to take place, seeing that no such thing happens in (a) and (b), and the structure that is input to the first step contains no OCP violation.

13. Interestingly, the OCP effect is only between the inserted [voice] and the sound to the right. Voice fill-in is not blocked if the *previous* syllable begins with a voiced sound:
   oko-go-ke-karaangera -> oko-go-ge-karaangera

CHAPTER 3

GLOTTALIZATION AND ASPIRATION

3.1 Overview of Laryngeal node neutralization

Glottalization and aspiration also participate in neutralization. The evidence proposed for the laryngeal node (Clements 1985) is the fact that languages with multiple laryngeal distinctions may neutralize all distinctions in certain positions. If the Voice Constraint is the correct analysis of voicing neutralization, it is expected that the neutralization of other laryngeal features would result from a constraint of a similar form, leading to the conclusion that there is a generalized Laryngeal Constraint.

Evidence was given in chapter 1 that glottalization and aspiration are marked by privative features that I call [gl] and [asp]. There are two important differences between these features and [voice] for the purposes of the Constraint. One difference is that while sonorants appear to be underspecified for [voice], they can be specified [gl] or [asp]. As expected, since sonorants can be marked for these features, they are also subject to neutralization in some languages. This will be examined in more detail in chapter 4. Also, the Voice Constraint mentions [+son]. If [voice] or other laryngeal features are licensed before [+son], what if that sonorant is glottalized or aspirated? This question will be addressed in the analysis of Klamath.

The other difference is that while voicing has a strong tendency to spread in obstruent clusters, the same does not appear to be true of [gl] and [asp]. Ancient Greek is supposed to have clusters that agree in aspiration, but otherwise this seems hardly to exist. I will argue that phonological double linking of [asp] does exist in other languages, such as Sanskrit, where the aspiration is phonetically realized only on the release of a cluster (or geminate). (Similar effects of multiply linked [gl] in clusters are predicted but at present I have no examples).

To begin, I will present evidence that neutralization can basically be analyzed with a constraint of the same form as the Voice Constraint. In languages with laryngeal distinctions other than voicing, the Constraint can take several forms. As I argued in the previous chapter, neutralized sounds have no Laryngeal node; there is no representation with a bare Laryngeal node, and neutralization delinks the entire node. Thus if a language has neutralization of all of its laryngeal features, what it has is a constraint on where an obstruent can have a Laryngeal node. One possibility is a language that has, say, voicing and aspiration in obstruents, and both are neutralized, as in Clements's example of Thai. In this case, the constraint can be stated as a constraint on where a Laryngeal node can occur: a Laryngeal node is only licensed in the configuration in (1):

(1)

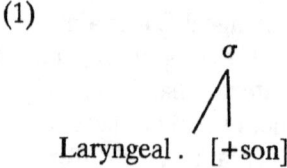

Laryngeal . [+son]

Some languages have more than one laryngeal distinction, but only one feature is neutralized. For instance, Tol and Hupa have voiceless, aspirated, and glottalized obstruents. Aspiration is neutralized, but glottalization is not. The constraint in this language, then, must mention the particular feature:

(2)

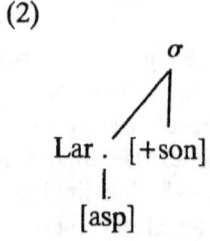

Lar . [+son]
 |
 [asp]

I will refer to the constraint from now on as the Laryngeal Constraint. This should be construed as meaning a constraint on the entire node, as in (1), unless specified.

Glottalization and Aspiration

The existence of such possibilities suggests that the statement of the Voice Constraint given in the previous chapter must be refined. Since the only laryngeal distinction in those languages is [voice], they actually have the constraint of the form given in (1). There is no need to specifically mention [voice] in the constraint if that is the only laryngeal feature in the language.

There is also no need to specify that [-son] is subject to the constraint for the languages in chapter 2. It would be redundant to specify this, since those languages have only voiced sonorants, which are unmarked for laryngeal features. The possibility of specifying that the Constraint applies to [-son] only arises in languages that have sonorants marked [gl] and [asp]. These sonorants are subject to the Constraint in some languages and not in others. In cases where sonorants do not obey the Constraint, it must be stated as applying to [-son]. In cases where they do obey the constraint, or where the language has no glottalized or aspirated sonorants, the constraint will be of the form in (1). This will be discussed in more detail in chapter 4.

The remainder of this section gives a brief description of languages that show evidence of the Constraint with various features. The rest of the chapter gives analyses in detail. This chapter deals with languages in which the Constraint applies to obstruents only. In all cases except that of Klamath this is because the language only has a laryngeal distinction in obstruents; the constraint is thus of the form in (1).

A simple example of a language that shows the Laryngeal Constraint is Maidu (Shipley 1956, 1963, 1964). The obstruent inventory of Maidu is given in (3).

(3)
 ɓ ɗ
 p' t' c' k'
 p t c k

In Maidu, syllable-final consonants cannot be implosive or glottalized. This is true of underlying forms, and there are also morphological alternations.

(4)
  a. /hyt'/ 'fat, grease'
             batam hyt'i   'butter'
             hytpe   'fat, obese'
  b. /pit'/ pit 'defecate; feces'
             pit'i k'atanoky   'manure-rolling beetle'
             pitk'ololo   'intestines'

Thus, the only type of consonant that can appear syllable-finally is voiceless: the consonant with no Laryngeal node. This is explained if Maidu has the Laryngeal Constraint: consonants with a Laryngeal node can only appear in the licensed configuration, which is syllable-initial.

Other languages that show the Laryngeal Constraint on the entire node are Korean, Klamath, Sanskrit and ancient Greek. The phonology of these will be analyzed in detail in the next section.

A language that has more than one laryngeal distinction and has the Laryngeal Constraint on only a single feature is Hupa. Hupa (Athabaskan; Woodward 1964) has voiceless, aspirated and glottalized stops. Syllable and word final stops may be only voiceless or glottalized; they may not be aspirated. The constraint in this language, then, is not on the entire Laryngeal node, but only on the feature [asp], as in (5).

(5)

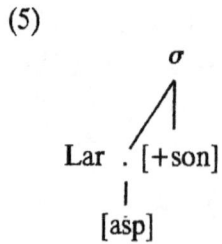

Other languages of this type are Tol, Bengali, and Marathi, discussed below. The existence of these languages is not evidence against the Laryngeal node, since in a large proportion of cases of neutralization, all laryngeal features are neutralized; cases where only one feature is neutralized seem to be less common (see the appendix to this chapter). If there were no node dominating the features, there would be no explanation for the fact that they usually pattern together.

Final Exceptionality must also be considered. Gujarati is a language that shows the Laryngeal Constraint on [asp] and has Final Exceptionality. The language has voiced, voiceless, voiced aspirated, and voiceless aspirated stops. Aspirated stops cannot occur at the end of word-internal syllables; alternations show that this is a productive process as well as a constraint on underlying form. Aspirated stops can occur word-finally, however. This is evidence of the constraint in (5) combined with Final Exceptionality. Bengali and Marathi are additional examples. (The details of Gujarati phonology will be discussed below.)

Tojolabal (Mayan; Supple and Douglass 1949, Furbee-Losee 1976) is another language with final exceptionality, to be discussed later.

In languages with aspiration and glottalization there can be some question as to whether a single aspirated segment or a consonant-/h/ cluster is involved. In some cases to be discussed, my interpretation differs from that the sources. Evidence for the phonemic analysis is discussed in the sections in question.

3.2 Constraint on the Laryngeal node

3.2.1 Thai

Thai has voiced, plain voiceless, and voiceless aspirated stops and affricates (Henderson 1949, Noss 1964, Clements 1985).[1]

(6)

b	d		g	
p	t	c	k	ʔ
p^h	t^h	c^h	k^h	
m	n		ŋ	
w	l,r	j		
f	s			h

The only obstruents that can appear syllable-finally are /k,t,p/ (and /ʔ/ according to Henderson). Thus Thai has the Laryngeal Constraint (1), as already mentioned above.

There are no morphophonemic alternations that show an active process of neutralization in Thai. The language is made up mostly of monosyllabic words, so the situations in which we would see alternations do not arise. Languages of this type provide an additional argument for formulating neutralization as a wellformedness constraint rather than as a rule of delinking. A rule of delinking suggests that at some level the distinctions exist, and that their absence on the surface is due to the action of a rule in a phonological derivation. However, there is no evidence in this language that the laryngeal distinctions ever appear syllable-finally, so it would be incorrect to account for the facts in this way. A wellformedness condition like the Laryngeal Constraint accounts for the distributional facts in such a language without invoking a derivational process for which there is no evidence.

3.2.2 Klamath

A number of questions must be decided before the operation of the Laryngeal Constraint in Klamath can be discussed. Section 3.2.2.1 will present arguments regarding the underlying phonological constrasts of the language. Section 3.2.2.2 will discuss the distribution of laryngeal contrasts in sonorants, arguing that they pattern differently from the obstruents and should not be included in considering the behavior of the Laryngeal Constraint. Finally, section 3.2.2.3 discusses the Laryngeal Constraint as it applies to obstruents in Klamath.

3.2.2.1 The phoneme system. Klamath (Barker 1964) has a three-way contrast in laryngeal features in both the stops and the sonorants: plain, aspirated, and glottalized. The phonemic transcriptions of Barker (1964) use symbols /p,b,p'/ to represent the distinctions. The allophone distribution to be analyzed is as follows (these are only positions where there is a distinction--in other positions the distinction is neutralized):

(7)
   #(C)__V: p^h p p'
   V,C__R: p b p'
   V__V, #__R:
      p less aspirated, b slightly long, p'

Glottalization and Aspiration

Barker's transcription suggests that /p/ and /b/ are distinguished by voicing, and Kingston (1985) assumes that the underlying stop system is as in Barker's transcription, with a voicing distinction. In fact, Barker could not have intended this interpretation, since under the assumptions of the structuralist framework to which he adheres, /p,b/ cannot be described as 'voiced' or 'voiceless' since phonemes are not phonetic objects. And there are a number of reasons to reject this system as an analysis of the underlying distinctions.

The most important objection is that the analysis of the obstruent system that assumes an aspiration distinction rather than a voicing distinction is required in order to make sense of the whole consonant system of the language, including the sonorants. Barker describes voiceless, voiced, and glottalized sonorants. The present theory requires that voiceless sonorants must be underlying aspirates; there is phonological evidence in this language (cited later) that this is correct. If Klamath has a distinction of aspiration in the stops, and the 'voiceless' sonorants are actually aspirated, then the sonorant system makes the same distinctions as the obstruent system, and only two laryngeal features are needed:

Feature	Stop	Sonorant
unmarked	voiceless	voiced
asp	aspirated	'voiceless'
gl	glottalized	glottalized

Although there is no theoretical requirement that consonant systems be symmetrical in this way, nevertheless they do seem to have this tendency. Under the theory that there is no feature [-voice], in order to represent the Barker/Kingston version of the Klamath system an additional feature is needed, [voice], used in the stops; also [asp] would be used in the sonorants and not the obstruents:

Feature	Stop	Sonorant
unmarked	voiceless	voiced
asp		'voiceless'
gl	glottalized	glottalized
voice	voiced	

This analysis not only requires more features, but it requires that the sonorants have an additional laryngeal distinction that the obstruent system does not employ. This would be highly unusual, as the tendency of languages is to have either the same or fewer laryngeal distinctions in sonorants as obstruents; it is not common for the sonorants to have more laryngeal distinctions. (For example, Maddieson (1984) includes no such languages; see the discussion in chapter 4.)

Additional evidence for the underlying aspiration of voiceless sonorants is available in Klamath.

There is evidence for aspiration from Barker's phonetic descriptions of the voiceless sonorants. He says that they are preaspirated and voiceless. This corresponds to the description of the glottalized sonorants, which are said to be preglottalized. Since glottalization is realized before closure and is clearly the realization of distinctive underlying glottalization, it is not unreasonable to interpret aspiration before closure in the same way, since it is phonologically distinctive.

More convincing is evidence from the phonology of Klamath that the voiceless sonorants are aspirated. This is argued by Clements (1985). Sequences of two laterals (including those in which the second lateral is derived by assimilation) undergo debuccalization of the second segment:

(8)
 ll̥ -> lh
 ll' -> l?

This rule results in only the laryngeal features of the second consonant remaining. [asp] results in [h], and [gl] in glottal stop. The details of this relationship between the laryngeal features and the laryngeal consonants are not entirely clear in current feature theory, but that the sort of correspondence shown here exists is an

Glottalization and Aspiration

unarguable fact, so this can be taken as supporting evidence that the voiceless sonorants are aspirates. The assumption that [h] and [?] are consonants consisting of only Laryngeal nodes, [asp] and [gl] respectively, will give the correct result for cases like this.

Another argument for the present analysis of the stop system is that the voiced allophones appear in voiced environments (intervocalic, before a plain voiced sonorant). The allophonic rules that would produce a voiced sound from a voiceless sound in these environments are unproblematic. Contrariwise, a rule to make a voiced sound into a voiceless allophone word-initial, as would be required under Barker's system, is more unnatural.

I will continue to transcribe the aspirated sonorants with symbols like /l̥ /, but it should be kept in mind that these symbols stand for sounds that are phonologically marked by the feature [asp].

3.2.2.2 Sonorants. Klamath has the Laryngeal Constraint: the three-way distinction in obstruents only occurs before a vowel or plain sonorant in the same syllable, which is the position licensed by the Constraint. Klamath also has some restrictions on the occurrence of the glottalized and aspirated sonorants, but these are separate, so before discussing the details of the Laryngeal Constraint, I will describe the distribution of sonorants, to show that these should not be included in the discussion. The sonorants are distributed as follows (Barker gives additional detail about the phonetic qualities of the allomorphs of the phonemes in different position, but here I am transcribing only the phonemic contrasts). Some refinements to this distributional statement will be made shortly.

Sonorants: Barker's description for nasals:
Contrast: 1. #(C)__V
         2. V__V
         3. V__C
No contrast: syllabic: 4. #__C
                      5. C__C
No contrast: 6. V__#

(9) Examples of each position:
```
   1. tmo         'grouse'
      mis         'you (sg. objective)'
      nis         'me'
      ṇaas        'one'
      m'aas?a     'tastes; is sick'
      n'aat'a     'Wilson snipe'
   2. gaama       'grinds'
      q'iṃaač     'ant'
      woṇa        'finishes'
      yam'a       'admires'
   3. č'omčaq     'bush,sp.'
      t'oṃt'oml'i 'flat on top'
      sqel'am'č   'Old Marten'
   4. m̥sas       'prairie dog'
      ṇč'ets      'bark'
      ŋkas        'stomach'
      ŋq'aq       'top of the head'
   5. gogm̥ča     'dist. get old'
      ?esŋk'a     'cries hard'
   6. som         'mouth'
      won         'elk'
```

(Other sonorants show basically the same distribution, with some additional complications of vowel-glide alternations. Final /l'/ is said to appear rarely, and there is one instance of final /y'/.)

(3) and Barker's charts of medial clusters show that there is a three-way distinction syllable-finally in the sonorants, unlike in the obstruents. The medial clusters with glottalized and aspirated first members are shown in (10):

(10)
```
   m'č  m'?  l̥b   l̥w   l̥y   l̥?   l̥q'  l̥W   l̥w'
   w̥ǰ  wp'  wk'  wq'  wl̥   wl'  y̥q'  ŋ̥w
   m̥tg ŋ̥tt' w̥tb  w̥tg  w̥qw'
```

When syllabic, nasals lose their laryngeal distinctions; presumably because only plain voiced nasals can be syllable peaks. Morphological alternations showing this are given by Kingston.

Glottalization and Aspiration

(11b) is a reduplicated form of (11a). The second instance of /l̥/, after the application of other rules, comes to stand between two consonants; here it must be syllabic (given Barker's description of the distribution of sonorant allophones), so it loses its aspiration and becomes voiced. (11c) shows the same phenomenon with a glottalized sonorant, /l'/.

(11)
  a. wl̥ ič'a 'shakes out'
  b. wl̥ iwl̥ča 'shake out dist.'
  c. sl'aba 'blooms' sl'as̩ba 'blooms dist.'

Leaving aside the syllabic sonorants, then, the distribution is that there is no contrast in word-final position, but there is a contrast in syllable-final position. This distribution cannot be accounted for by the Laryngeal Constraint, which would rule out aspiration and glottalization both syllable and word finally, nor by the Constraint and Final Exceptionality, which would allow the contrast word-finally but not syllable-finally.

The distribution of glottalized sonorants also does not accord with the behavior of cases of the Laryngeal Constraint. Final clusters can contain glottalized sonorants that are not the final segment of the cluster:

(12)
  m'ol's   'pus'
  moon's   'big one'
  čiyaal's   'salmon'
  ?ool's   'dove'
  wt'am's   'lid, top'

The Laryngeal Constraint would rule out these glottalized sonorants in final clusters as well as those in absolute word-final position, so the word-final restriction must be the result of some other constraint or rule. An additional restriction on glottalized sonorants in clusters is that the following segment must be [+cont]. (Except the medial cluster /m'?/ in the table; I have no explanation for this.) Barker (p53) states that glottalized sonorants are neutralized before another consonant, except that they remain glottalized before /s,č/ (thus, before [+cont] segments, following Lombardi (1990a,b) on the representation of the affricate). (12) above shows these clusters word-finally, and the examples in (13) show that such clusters are possible medially (including some clusters not in Barker's lists).[2]

(13)
?on'če   'later, soon, after a while' (dict.,39)
wt'am'sl'iiya 'makes, gets a lid for it' (456)
sw'aal'sgen   'Piled-Up-Place (name)' (399)

Sonorants deglottalize before a segment that is not [+cont] regardless of syllable constituency: both within a coda, and in a coda before the initial consonant of the next syllable. They do not deglottalize if the following segment is [+cont][3]:

(14)
/wt'am̩'/   'make a lid'
wt'am'sl'iiya 'makes, gets a lid for it' (456)
wt'ambli   'put a lid back on'
wt'am's   'lid, top'

/waqn'a/   'boy's voice changes'
wagantk

go?ool'as   'tadpole'
go?oolk'a   'little tadpole'

čiyaal's   'salmon'
čičiyaalk'a   'dist. little salmon'

Since the facts are the same whether R' is within a syllable or between syllables, this is a linear constraint that does not refer to syllable constituency. Thus the constraint on glottalized sonorants is: they are licensed before [+cont]. They will neutralize--that is, lose [gl]--when standing before a segment that is not [+cont], because [gl] will not be licensed.

Glottalized sonorants are also licensed before vowels, since the three-way contrast is possible there. Given these two positive constraints, a negative constraint on word-final glottalized sonorants is unnecessary; they will deglottalize there because it is

Glottalization and Aspiration

not one of the licensed positions, since a consonant that is word-final obviously does not precede [+cont]. Ito (1986) demonstrates that negative and positive constraints are formally equivalent. However, in many cases only the positive statement of the constraint is consistent with other aspects of phonological theory. For example, Ito gives a negative constraint on [-cor] in Lardil, but this cannot be the true statement of the constraint if [cor] is a privative feature. The constraint on glottalized sonorants in Klamath is also an licensing constraint that must be stated positively, not negatively. We cannot have a constraint that forbids a glottalized sonorant before a [-cont] segment, because the affricate /č/ is [-cont], and R' is permitted there. (For the same reason, a rule of deglottalization will not work).

Aspirated sonorants are prohibited only absolutely word finally; Barker gives one example of a final cluster with an aspirated sonorant, /lʰ t/, and several in the medial clusters ((10) above). This seems to be the only constraint on their appearance, and so this cannot be reanalyzed as the result of a positive constraint on where they are licensed. Such word-edge restrictions are not uncommon (for instance, English and Hupa (Bright 1986) have no [ŋ] word-initially, and Bhojpuri (Shukla 1981) no aspirated sonorants) and it is plausible that many of these are simply negative constraints.

To sum up, then, glottalized sonorants are subject to certain licensing conditions, but not to the Laryngeal Constraint. The Constraint therefore must be restricted to obstruents, having the form in (15c), and the additional constraints in (15a,b) are also part of Klamath grammar:

(15)
a. Aspirated sonorants are forbidden word-finally:
  *[+son]#
      |
     asp

b. Glottalized sonorants are only permitted before vowel or [+cont]:
Positive constraints:

  [+son] [+cont]   [+son] V
     | |
     gl   gl

c.
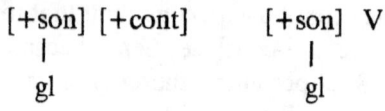

More discussion of languages with the constraint in (15c) can be found in Chapter 4.

3.2.2.3 Obstruents. Having demonstrated that the sonorants are not subject to the Laryngeal Constraint I will now examine the Laryngeal Constraint as it applies to obstruents in Klamath. (Except where it is crucial I have retained Barker's transcriptions, which use voiceless and voiced instead of aspirated and voiceless consonants.) Barker described the distribution as follows (O = obstruent, R = sonorant):

Contrast:
 1. #(C)__V
 2. V__V
 3. V,C__R
 4. #__R
No contrast:
 5. V,C__O
 6. #__O
 7. V(C)__#

Glottalization and Aspiration

Here I have retained Barker's transcriptions except in boldface where I give the contrasting phonemes as I have analyzed them-- voiceless, aspirated and glottalized.)

1. **pʰeč** 'foot'
   peqsa 'grinds with mortar and pestle'
   p'elq'a 'licks'
   k**pʰoč**'a 'chases away'
   k**peewa** 'orders, commands'
   k**p'eq**'a 'hits in the face with fist'
2. t'a**pʰ**aq 'leaf'
   sl'a**pa** 'bloom'
   q'osa**p'**as 'pocketknife'
3. ma**kʰ**lga 'camps at'
   nči**k'**lga 'drips down'
   wdo**k**lgi 'comes to beat someone'
4. **tʰ**laqs 'mullet, sp.'
   tlol 'cricket'
   t'loqs 'basket hopper'

In these examples of the positions where there is no contrast, the neutralized stop is in boldface.

5. ge**p**ga 'comes'
   nči**k**ta 'drips on'
6. **t**q'op'o 'thumb'
   ptipsap 'father'
   q?is 'rattlesnake'
7. ne**p** 'hand'
   we**q** 'arm'
   nga**k** 'turtle'

1-4 are positions where the obstruent is before a vowel, or is in a obstruent-sonorant onset cluster. These are the positions licensed by the Laryngeal Constraint.

(7) is word-final position; this is unlicensed and neutralizes as expected. (Barker describes these as aspirated, I assume this means they are released, not distinctively marked [asp] The justification for this is the same as given for Tol: see section 3.2.2 below). (6), word-initial before an obstruent, is not in the licensed

configuration, as it is not presonorant. Clements and Keyser argue that these are extrasyllabic, and Steriade that they are attached directly to the syllable node. In either case they will not be in the licensed configuration, and as expected, there are no laryngeal distinctions in this position. In cases like (5), regardless of the syllable affiliation of the obstruents--whether they are syllable-final, extrasyllabic, or part of an initial obstruent-obstruent cluster--they will not be in the licensed configuration, so that the details of syllabification are not crucial. The only crucial aspect of the syllable structure is that the consonant is not in an onset before a more sonorous segment, so it cannot have laryngeal features.

I have discussed the problems with the analysis of Kingston (1985, 1990) earlier, but one of his points, that laryngeal constrasts in obstruents are only possible in onset position, is correct, and this is what the Laryngeal Constraint captures. It should be noted that this analysis works regardless of the analysis of the phoneme system of Klamath; the distinctions occur only where licensed, regardless of which distinctions you analyze the language as having.

Another important aspect of Kingston's analysis has to do with syllabification. (See also Clements and Keyser 1983). The distributional statements given are the surface generalizations--the Constraint in Klamath is operative on surface syllabification. Kingston shows that some rules require a different syllabification early in the derivation. The Laryngeal Constraint is not operative on this earlier syllabification (thus Klamath is not like German, where the underlying syllabification determines the facts of neutralization; rather the neutralization facts are surface generalizations, as in most of the other languages I discuss.) Kingston argues that OR clusters must be first syllabified in separate syllables, because otherwise the rules of vowel deletion will not work properly. After vowel deletion, these are resyllabified as complex onsets. The Constraint does not apply to the first level of syllabification, so that underlying (16a) does not lose its glottalization, and surfaces after resyllabification as (16b):

3.2.3 Korean

The fact that Korean has syllable-final neutralization is uncontroversial, so it is clearly a language with the Laryngeal Constraint. The following examples from Kim-Reynaud (1977) show this (I have omitted the results of an additional rule, Post-Obstruent Tensing):

(17)
/apʰ/   [ap]   'front'
/apʰ-to/   [apto]   'front also'

/k'ək'-ta/ [kəkta]   'breaks off'
/k'ək'-ə/   [k'ək'ə] 'Break it off'

The difficulty for some authors is not the neutralization, but what the features of the stop system are. It has sometimes been described as containing plain voiceless, 'lightly aspirated' and 'heavily aspirated' stops.[4] This is clearly an impossibility under my feature system, as well as under most feature systems that are based on cross-linguistic data. The study of Abramson and Lisker (1972), using synthesized speech presented to native speakers of Korean, showed that voice onset time was not sufficient to distinguish the three categories of Korean stops; since VOT is a correlate of aspiration, this seems to be additional evidence that this is not two varieties of aspiration. In fact, the correct description of Korean is that it has glottalized, plain and aspirated stops, as a number of authors have assumed. Ladefoged (1983) says that the fortis stops have 'a slight degree of laryngealization' (p.354). Ladefoged (1973) categorizes the Korean stops in question as the same as glottalized stops, describing them as 'voiceless fortis plosive;' he mentions that a slight degree of laryngealization may be heard in the vowel preceding one of these consonants. Martin (1951) refers to a Korean phonetician, Jung, who calls these stops implosive, and a Japanese linguist, Ogura, who writes them preglottalized. Martin says that he hears distinct glottal tension although the sounds are not as strongly glottalized as many American Indian languages. Young-Seok Kim (1985) classifies the sounds as [+cg] for the purposes of his morphological study.

Thus a number of writers assume the analysis of the Korean system as consisting of voiceless, aspirated and glottalized stops, but some do not. The main problem appears to be the fact that phonetic realization of the glottalized stops is somewhat unusual; they are not the usual ejective glottalic stops of other languages. In particular the phonetic work of Kim (1965, 1970) attempts to argue that these are not glottalized stops.

Kim (1965, 1970) argues that these stops are not glottalized, because his cineradiographic investigations show that the glottis is never completely closed in these stops, and it is not the same mechanism as ejectives. Nevertheless, his diagrams show the glottis very nearly closed; these stops have the narrowest glottal constriction of the three series in Korean. The fiberoptic study of Kagaya (1974) shows that the fortis stops have completely adducted, stiff, but not vibrating vocal cords. The electromyographic study of Hirose, Lee and Ushijima (1974) showed that these stops involved tension of the vocal folds and constriction of the glottis. The vocalis (VOC) and lateral cricoarytenoid (LCA) muscles showed activation in these stops. They note that activity of the interarytenoid (INT) muscles did not correlate with VOC and LCA, although these are often considered to be the adductor muscles; significantly for my position, LCA and VOC show activity and INT does not in glottal stop production and in Danish stod, both uncontroversial examples of glottal constriction. Lisker and Abramson (1972) note that some speakers have "quite audible vocal fry or laryngealization" in these stops.

All of this points to the conclusion that these sounds are indeed 'constricted glottis'. The feeling of 'tenseness' that is so salient to native speakers is undoubtedly the tenseness of the glottal constriction, and it is not necessary to postulate any other phonological feature to account for it. As discussed in chapter 1, different phonetic realizations are possible for various laryngeal contrasts; for instance, creaky voiced and voiced implosive stops never contrast, and should be considered phonologically the same.

Glottalization and Aspiration

Kingston (1985) shows that the production of ejectives not only varies among languages (Quiche and Tigrinya) but also among several speakers of the same language; see also Pinkerton (1986). Lindau (1982) shows that implosives are not phonetically the same in all languages.

Thus it seems quite reasonable to consider the Korean fortis stops as phonologically marked [gl], but with a somewhat unusual phonetic realization. It is certainly more reasonable than proposing a whole new feature or feature system for the sake of Korean only. Of course, no matter what the stop system of Korean, the Laryngeal Constraint will still give the correct results for neutralization, since there is little argument that the contrasts, whatever they are, appear only in syllable-initial position.

Kim-Reynaud analyzes Korean syllable-final neutralization as a result of the fact that syllable-final stops are not released. The problems with this type of analysis are discussed at the end of chapter 2 and at the end of this chapter, in the analysis of Kingston's binding theory.

Korean has additional phonology involving the laryngeal features that does not have a direct bearing on the questions I am investigating, for example a rule usually called Post-Obstruent Tensing--under the present analysis of the stop system it should be called Post-Obstruent Glottalization. Although the exact environment for the rule must take into account various complications about morphological boundaries that I will not go into, the process is basically quite simple, that an obstruent becomes glottalized after another obstruent. Thus the surface forms of the examples in (17) are as given in (18):

(18)
/ap^h/   [ap]   'front'
/ap^h-to/   [apt'o]   'front also'

/k'ək-ta/   [kəkt'a]   'breaks off'
/k'ək-ə/   [k'ək'ə]   'Break it off'

[-son] [-son] -> [-son] [-son]
                              |
                            [gl]

This rule does not apply if the second stop is aspirated. This is to be expected since [asp] and [gl] cannot combine in a single sound.

(19) /cək-tʰo/   [cəktʰo] 'red dirt'

3.3 Constraint on single features

3.3.1 Bengali, Marathi

Bengali (Ferguson and Chowdhury 1960, Ferguson 1945) has voiceless, voiced, voiced aspirated and voiceless aspirated stops. (The aspirated labials are often realized as fricatives.) Word-finally, there is no aspiration contrast, but voiced stops are possible:

(20)
    meg 'cloud'
    roḍ 'road'

Thus Bengali has the Constraint on aspiration only. This is confirmed by the consonant cluster facts: voiced-voiceless clusters are possible, so there is no neutralization of voicing. There is spreading of voice, since there are no voiceless-voiced clusters.

(21)

pp	pt	pṭ	pc	ps	pk	
bb	bt	bd	bṭ	bc	bh	bg
tt	tṭ	ts	tk			
dd	dṭ	ds	dk			
ṭt	ṭṭ	ṭc	ṭk			
ḍḍ						
cb	cṭ	cc	ck			
jp	jb	jt	jṭ	jj	jk	
ky	kṭ	kc	ks	kk		
gb	gt	gd	gṭ	gc	gg	

(Ferguson and Chowdhury do not explicitly state that these are only morpheme-internal clusters, but one might infer that they are, since in their discussion of the clusters they feel the need to make excuses for their use of the 'dynamic' word 'assimilation.')

Morphological alternations show that voice also spreads in the phonology, but only between homorganic stops (22a), except in the case of the velar (22b), which varies between voiced and voiceless before a voiced stop (from Ferguson 1945):[5]

(22) a.   b.
   map 'measure'   mabbo   'I will measure'
   hat 'hard'   dhɔra 'grasped'   haddhɔra 'under one's control'
   pãc 'five'   jon 'people'   pãjjor   'five people'
   ḍak 'mail'   ghɔr 'house'   ḍagghɔr 'post office'
  b.
   thak 'remain'   thakbo ~ thagbo 'I will remain'

Marathi is probably also a language with the constraint on aspiration only, not voicing. It has the same four-stop series as Bengali. Houlihan and Iverson (1979) give the following data showing neutralization of final aspiration, but not voicing.

(23)
   tap   'fever'   tapala 'to the fever'
   top   'cannon'   tophela 'to the cannon'
   vad   'discussion'   vadala 'to the discussion'
   dud   'milk'   dudhala 'to the milk'

I have no data on consonant clusters in this language. (An informant that I consulted did not have final deaspiration; I assume that this is a dialect difference.)

3.3.2 Tol

Tol (Hokan; Fleming and Dennis 1977) has voiceless, aspirated, and glottalized stops, but syllable-finally there are only glottalized and plain. Thus Tol has the same constraint as given in (5) for Hupa.

    Alternations given in (24) show that underlying aspiration is neutralized word-finally.

(24)
sit	sit^{h}in	'avocado'
c'ec	cec^{h}em	'tortilla'
lup	lup^{h}uk	'hail'

According to Fleming and Dennis, nearly all nouns are of this type, but there are two examples with underlying unaspirated consonants:

(25)
kep	kepan	'woman'
sipip	sipis	'pigeon'[6]

Although the lack of plain voiceless final nouns is unusual, they are clear both that there is a phonemic contrast syllable-initially, and that there is no contrast of plain and aspirated syllable-finally. The latter statement is made several times, although unfortunately no chart of medial clusters is given. The phonemic distinction can be illustrated by minimal pairs and near-minimal pairs:

(26)
pe	'rock'		pɨʔɨ	'he is lying down'
p^{h}e	'white'		p^{h}ɨ	'all'

The fact that glottalization is not subject to the constraint is illustrated by the following words.[7]

(27)
mac'	moc'ik	'toasted corn drink'
cec'	cec'em	'giant'
wɨt'	wɨt'is	'firewood'

Word-finally and preceding a consonant other than a stop, the glottalized consonants "may have a delayed release, a voiceless release, or a voiced short vowel release." This might suggest an alternative analysis wherein there is a vowel at some point in the phonological derivation, and glottalization is preserved because it is in an onset preceding this vowel. This analysis is untenable, because the glottalization distinction is also preserved before a stop, and in this case "all three series of stops are released into the

Glottalization and Aspiration

following consonant without a detectable transition sound." It appears, in fact, that stops are not released in this position, another blow to the theory that release is necessary for glottal contrasts, since the glottalization distinction is preserved here. The glottalized series is realized in this position by "laryngealization of the preceding vowel and by glottal closure for the consonant articulation."

In addition, they describe initial glottalized consonants as sometimes being realized as plain, followed by a short laryngealized vowel and glottal stop. This clearly seems to be a property of phonetic realization, with no justification for positing an additional underlying vowel. If a underlying vowel is posited for the case of word-final consonants, word-initial consonants would need an entirely different generalization. However, we can account for both cases by saying that this is a possible realization of released glottalized stops. This preserves the generalization between initial and final stops, and explains their difference from unreleased pre-consonantal stops. In any case, it is clearly in the domain of phonetic realization and not the underlying phonological representation.

A final point that must be made is that Fleming and Dennis transcribe all word-final nonglottalized stops as aspirates, saying that they have "at least some degree of aspiration". A language that allowed aspirated and glottalized stops word-finally but did not allow voiceless stops would be highly unusual. But if the final nonglottalized stops are interpreted as plain voiceless, with the "some degree of aspiration" constituting simply the release of the stop, this language has the normal type of neutralization. Thus I have reinterpreted their transcriptions, writing word-final stops as plain instead of aspirated. The importance of this is that we do not want the theory to allow neutralization to a marked category unless there is overwhelming evidence that languages allow this, since it complicates the theory. If neutralization can result in aspirated stops, then it must be delinking of any features present and insertion of [asp]. If this is possible, we expect to find neutralization to glottalized stops and neutralization to voiced stops. But this is unknown. In all other cases, neutralization results in plain voiceless stops. Since it seems likely that the authors have simply erroneously identified the release of the final stop with aspiration, Tol does not constitute evidence for making this major complication to the theory.

3.4 Constraint and Final Exceptionality

3.4.1 Tojolabal

Tojolabal, a Mayan language (Supple and Douglass 1949; also Furbee-Losee 1976), has a contrast between plain and glottalized stops. Supple and Douglass call the plain series aspirate, although their phonemic transcription uses plain voiceless symbols. They say that the allophones are aspirated in final position and unaspirated in initial or medial position; the examples for medial position are intervocalic. It appears that what they are calling 'aspiration' is not distinctive aspiration marked by the feature [asp], but the release of the consonant when there is no following vowel. Unless given this interpretation, the language has a system consisting of aspirated and glottalized stops, which is otherwise unknown. Furbee-Losee calls the stops plain and aspirated with no mention of aspiration in the language.

They state that all consonants can appear in syllable initial position and word-finally.

(28)
    potot'   'class of plant'
    c'okop'   'thread'
    ?ak'   'reed'
    soc'   'owl'

However, glottalized consonants cannot close a word-internal syllable. This shows that Tojolabal does have the Laryngeal Constraint, and that it has Final Exceptionality, since word-final consonants escape the constraint. The constraint is only on the feature [gl], but since this is the only distinctive laryngeal feature in the language, it is actually a constraint on the node.

3.4.2 Gujarati

Gujarati has voiceless, voiced, voiceless aspirated, and voiced aspirated stops. However, many writers analyze it as a language with Ch clusters instead of aspirates, following Pandit (1957). Pandit's justification for this analysis seems mainly to be based on

Glottalization and Aspiration

some facts about murmured vowels, as well as the impulse to reduce the size of the consonant inventory that is common to writers prior to the use of distinctive features. A later analysis, Modi (1986), argues that instead /h/ should be analyzed as an autosegment. Modi also claims that Pandit's data mixes two incompatable dialects, one in which murmur spreads to vowels and one in which it does not. I will confine my discussion to relevant aspects of the consonant phonology here. Cardona (1965) follows Pandit's analysis, but is the only source that gives enough phonological information. I will show, using Cardona's facts, that Gujarati should be analyzed as having single-segment voiced and voiceless aspirates like related languages, and then will discuss the Laryngeal Constraint in this language.

In a sequence VCCV, the syllable break is VC.CV (29a), unless the second consonant is h (or y); then it is V.CCV (29b). This makes sense if Ch is actually a single consonant.

(29)
a. šək.to   'able'   nəb.l̥o 'weak'
   jag.to   'waking'
b. a.bhar   'thanks'
   kɑ.phi   'coffee'
   cɑ.tho   'fourth'

The sequence stop-/h/ does not close a syllable. This makes sense if aspirates are single segments and Gujarati has the Laryngeal Constraint on [asp]; aspiration will then be neutralized in this position.

In initial three-consonant clusters, if the first is a stop, the second must be /h/. In fact, these are the only initial three-consonant cluster except for /skh, smr/. If aspirates are single segments, then we can say that there are no three-consonant clusters at all: the "three-consonant" clusters are aspirates followed by another consonant, or /sk^h/. The only exception to this is then /smr/, and it is common cross-linguistically for /s/ to have special properties as the first element of an initial cluster.

Cardona describes a phonological rule whereby ChC -> CC if the first consonant is a stop and the second is stop, spirant, or nasal. As he describes it this rule is totally random, but if Ch is analyzed as an aspirate, this is simply syllable-final deaspiration.

Given the single-segment analysis of Gujarati Ch clusters, we see the following:

Syllable-final aspirated stops deaspirate:
/ləkhto/ -> ləkto 'writing'
/ləkhnar/ -> ləknar 'writer'
Word-final aspirated stops are permitted:
/wag^h/ 'tiger', /dud^h/ milk, /lak^h/ 'a lac'.

Thus the language has the Laryngeal Constraint on [asp], and final exceptionality. Cardona gives examples like the following:

(30)
/uḍtalis/ '48'
/jag.to/ 'waking'

Although these are given in phonemic transcription, he makes no mention of devoicing or voice agreement, so syllable-final voiced stops appear to be permitted. Pandit (1965) says that there is voice assimilation in homorganic stops, which results in geminates, but otherwise there is no evidence of voice effects in stops in general. Thus the constraint is on the single feature, not the entire node.

Gujarati also has sonorant-/h/ clusters, but there is no evidence that these are single voiced aspirate segments. This kind of consonant system, with voiced aspirate obstruents but no aspirated sonorants, is not uncommon--Sanskrit is another example. The writing system used for both languages agrees with this analysis, having single graphemes for aspirated stops, but not for aspirated sonorants. Some suggestion that they might be single segments comes from the fact that /yh/ and /wh/ can be tautosyllabic: /layh.ri/ 'boasting,' /bawhro/ 'confused'. If these are single segments, the Laryngeal Constraint applies only to obstruents in this language.[8]

3.5 Spreading of aspiration

3.5.1 Sanskrit

Sanskrit (data from Whitney 1885, 1889 unless otherwise noted) has voiceless, voiced, and voiceless and voiced aspirated stops. It is

Glottalization and Aspiration

a language with the Laryngeal Constraint, as can be seen from the fact that it has final neutralization of voice and aspiration.

(31)
    /agnimat^h/   agnimat
    /viirud^h/   viirut
    /suhṛd/   suhṛt
    /triṣṭub^h/   triṣṭup

Clusters also show devoicing and deaspiration, as expected.

(32)   /adsi/   atsi

Clusters also must agree in voice:

(33)   /šakd^{h}i/   šagd^{h}i

(Voicing assimilation between words has different properties, and will be treated in Chapter 4.)

    In Sanskrit, a root can never have more than one voiced aspirate, but the environment determines which consonant of the root the aspiration appears on. The traditional controversy argues about whether these roots have one final aspirated consonant, whose aspiration moves in some cases, or two aspirated consonants, one of which deaspirates in some cases. I will not review this literature, since most of the controversy therein relating to rule ordering is irrelevant in light of the analysis I will propose. I assume that the roots have only one aspirate, and the analysis is most similar to the autosegmental treatment of Borowsky and Mester (1983).

    The results of Grassmann's Law (throwback of aspiration) and Bartholomae's law ("transfer" of aspiration) are shown in (34) (examples from Borowsky and Mester).

(34) root /budh/ "to know"
   a. bodhati   3rd sg pres ind
   b. bubodha   3rd sg perf
Throwback of aspiration (Grassmann's Law):
   c. bhotsyati   3rd sg fut
   d. abhutsi   1st sg aorist
   e. bhut   root noun, nom sg
   f. bhudbhis   root noun, instr pl
   g. bhuddhvam   2nd pl pres imp
Transfer of aspiration (Bartholomae's Law):
   h. buddha   past participle

Aspiration appears on the second consonant of the root in (a,b). It appears on the first consonant of the root in (c-g); these are the cases of aspiration throwback or Grassmann's Law (GL). (In f,g the suffixes also begin with an aspirate.) It appears in (h) after a consonant cluster at the end of the root, and not on any root consonant. Here aspiration appears to have moved from the first consonant in the cluster to the second; these are the cases of Bartholomae's Law (BL).

Since Sanskrit has the Laryngeal Constraint, the root-final consonants in (34c-e) cannot be aspirated, as they are not in the licensed position; in these cases, the aspiration appears on the first consonant of the root. (34f,g) are cases where voice has assimilated. Since voice assimilation is a combination of neutralization and spreading, these are also cases where deaspiration has taken place. (This is essentially the insight of Borowsky and Mester 1983 restated in terms of the present theory). As expected, then, (f,g) behave like (c-e): aspiration appears on the first consonant. The only rule needed, given the existence of the Laryngeal Constraint, is the rule that associates the delinked feature to the root-initial consonant: Associate [asp]. This rule only applies within the root--[asp] will not associate to a consonant in a suffix or prefix (including reduplicated prefixes, which never contain aspirates). The roots in question have only one other consonant, so the rule need not be any more detailed.

Glottalization and Aspiration

The derivations of the forms (34c,e) are as follows.

(35)

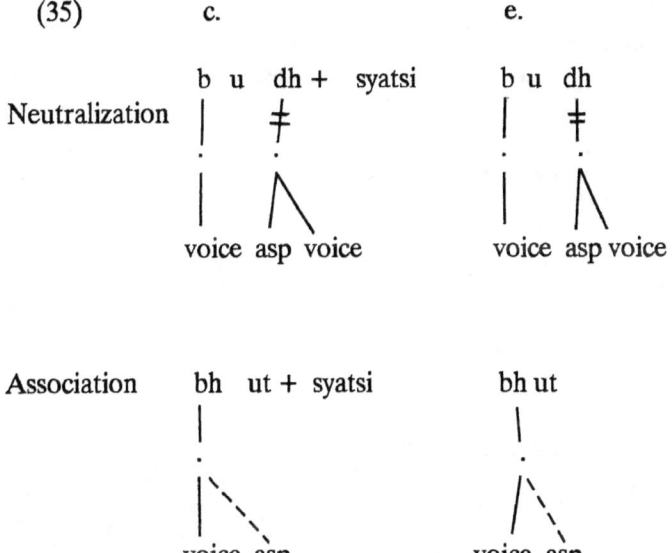

f.

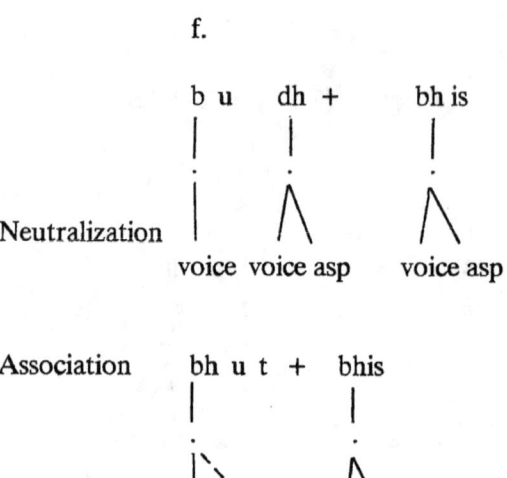

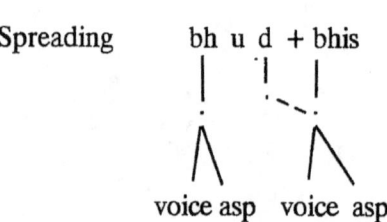

(The details of the spreading rule will be discussed shortly.)

The cases examined so far are relatively straightforward. The unusual cases are those like (h), where the aspiration has "transferred" to the following consonant. This is the environment for Progressive assimilation.

Progressive assimilation takes place when a root ends in a voiced aspirate and a suffix begins in /t/ or /t^h/:

(36)
$g^h + t \to gd^h$
$g^h + t^h \to gd^h$
$d^h + t \to dd^h$ $bud^h + ta \to budd^ha$
$d^h + t^h \to dd^h$ $rund^h + t^has \to rundd^has$
$b^h + t \to bd^h$ $lab^h + ta \to labd^ha$

Glottalization and Aspiration

In this case the entire cluster becomes voiced, and it looks like aspiration is transferred to the last consonant of the cluster. This could be analyzed as follows: deaspirate the final consonant of the root; spread voice to the right; relink aspiration to the rightmost consonant. This is rather complex and ad hoc. Instead, if some facts about aspiration in clusters are taken into account, this can be analyzed as progressive spread of the Laryngeal node, with aspiration being realized on the release of the entire cluster.

The facts to consider have to do with the behavior of aspiration in geminates. Languages that have geminate consonants and aspirates also have geminate aspirates, and these are always of the form CCh, not ChCh. This is true in Sanskrit: for instance, in circumstances where a consonant is supposed to be doubled, a aspirate becomes CCh. Interestingly, Whitney says that rare geminates are sometimes spelled ChCh instead, which seems to indicate that these are seen to be geminated aspirates. Evidence from other languages points to the same conclusion, for instance Hindi: CCh clusters appear to be traditionally considered to be geminates. They must be geminate or else they would violate two generalizations about Hindi: Homorganic stops do not cluster, and aspirates are never the second stop in a stop cluster (Ohala 1983). In Greek, clusters assimilate in voice and aspiration, unless they are otherwise identical consonants, in which case the cluster is CC^h; this is not an exception to the assimilation facts if this is actually a geminate aspirate. (Greek is analyzed in detail in the next section).

The phonological evidence, then, seems to indicate that these clusters consist of the root node of a [voice], [asp] sound, connected to two skeletal positions. The fact that only the second stop seems to be aspirated in these languages is due to the fact that aspiration is phonetically realized on the release of a stop. This is somewhat less the case when voiced aspirates are considered --"murmur" can be coextensive with stop closure--but even in the latter, however, one of the things distinguishing the sound is the period of breathy voice at the release of the closure. In a geminate, there is no release between the two consonants; thus, aspiration is realized on the release of the entire geminate. This is similar to geminate affricates: /cc/, for example, sounds like [tts]. The closure period is long, and then the fricative release is at the end; geminate affricates are never realized as [tsts] (Lombardi

1990a). Affricates and aspirates are similar in that the surface ordering--stop-fricative, closure-aspiration--is never distinctive, and is underlyingly unordered; the surface ordering is an aspect of phonetic realization. As geminates they also behave the same way: the closure period is lengthened, with one release only.

These facts about geminates must be kept in mind when analyzing languages with aspirates. For example, in Dhangar-Kurux (Gordon 1976) aspirates are permitted word-finally. The only medial clusters are homorganic nasal-stop clusters, geminates, and geminate aspirates. Since the latter are written /C.C^h/, on superficial examination this might look like a language with neutralization (and Final Exceptionality): the syllable-final stop is never aspirated in the transcription. But these should be analyzed as geminates, and since there are no other stop clusters there is no evidence for neutralization in this language.

Thus, the evidence from geminates shows that in a representation where a laryngeal node with [asp] is linked to two slots, [asp] may be phonetically realized only on the release of the second consonant. In the case of geminates, the entire Root node is linked to two skeletal positions. In the case of clusters, the Laryngeal node would be doubly linked to two Root nodes, but it does not seem unreasonable to assume that the effect would be the same. The phonological facts about the interaction of BL and GL support this, as I will show.

This interpretation of aspirate clusters allows the interaction of BL and GL to be accounted for with only one rule: the rule that spreads the laryngeal node of a root-final voiced aspirate to a suffix-initial coronal:

Glottalization and Aspiration

(37)

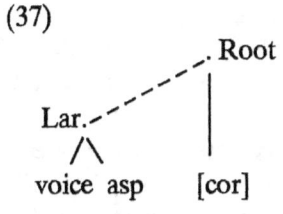

b u C C a = buddha
  \/
   |
  [voice]
  [asp]

The resulting cluster will be realized with aspiration only on its release, as reflected in the spelling, although it is not unlikely that it was murmured throughout. Recall that throwback of aspiration only occurs when [asp] becomes delinked from the second consonant. Since there is no deaspiration in these cases, there is no throwback of aspiration; no additional rule is needed.

I have shown that the rule of Progressive Assimilation that applies with some suffixes must be spread of the entire node, to account for the facts about GL in these forms. The next question is, does Sanskrit spread the whole Laryngeal node in regressive assimilation, as well as progressive? That is, in (38), is the whole cluster linked to [voice] and [asp], as in (37)?

(38) /šakd^{h}i/   šagd^{h}i

Evidence from other suffixes shows that this multiple linking must be true of these clusters as well. There is no aspiration throwback in (39):

(39)   /dugh/ -dhi   dugdhi

This is expected given the proposal about Fusion that is described in Chapter 2 with reference to Dutch. There must be fusion of the laryngeal nodes of the two voiced aspirates here. If the last consonant of the root neutralized and was later revoiced and reaspirated by the spreading rule, we could expect throwback of aspiration, since neutralization always results in throwback in this language. But there is no throwback, so the evidence shows that there was no neutralization.

An exception to the fusion of voiced aspirates are cases like (34f,g), *bhuddhvam, bhudbhis*. The endings /-dhvam/, /-dhve/ and /-bhis/ condition throwback, although other voiced-aspirate initial endings such as /-dhi/ do not, as shown in (39). /-bhis/ has a word boundary before it (Sag 1976, Borowsky and Mester 1983). In this case, deaspiration would indeed take place on the word cycle before the ending was added, causing throwback. The voice agreement in the cluster must then be a result of the spreading that is part of Sanskrit external sandhi. It cannot be proposed that /-dhvam/, /-dhve/ are preceded by a word boundary like /-bhis/ , because of the evidence of other rules; these are simply exceptional (see Sag 1976 p613, Schindler 1976 p 634-5).

A remaining question is why only voiced aspirates are involved in GL. If voiced aspirates are indeed marked with the feature [asp] rather than a separate feature like "murmur", why does GL only apply in cases where both root consonants are voiced--why is aspiration never thrown back onto a voiceless consonant to make a voiceless aspirate? This question is probably moot, given the distribution of sounds in the language. Whitney (1889) says: "Practically...the rules as to changes of aspirates concern only the sonant aspirates, since the surd, being of later development and rarer occurrence, are hardly ever found in situations that call for their occurrence." (p53) Whitney (1885) gives all the derivatives found in the texts he consulted. The roots in question are of the following forms:

    plain voiced-voiceless aspirate
    plain voiceless-voiceless aspirate
    plain voiceless-voiced aspirate

The texts simply do not contain forms of these roots in situations that would show throwback of aspiration. In many cases, the root takes a vowel-initial allomorph of a suffix, so that no deaspiration takes place. The only possible case is the root /krudh/, for which the forms /krotsyati/ and /cukrutsa-/ are given; but these forms are bracketed as not coming from the original texts. Whitney says that these forms are from the Hindu grammarians "as reported by Western authorities." Whitney seems to think that these sources are reliable. The rule that reassociates the unassociated laryngeal feature could certainly be written so that it only links to a voiced consonant, but it hardly seems worthwhile to complicate the analysis on the basis of only these two slightly doubtful forms.

Reduplicated consonants in Sanskrit are not aspirated even when the original consonant is an aspirate (40a), although there is no such effect between prefixes and roots (40b) (examples from Mester 1986):

(40)
   a. b^hid 'to split'   bib^{h}id
   b.   ab^{h}i-d^{h}a 'tell, speak'

Many analyses account for this as a case of Grassmann's Law, but not all; for example Sag (1974) argues that this is a spurious generalization, and Borowsky and Mester propose that the reduplication template is prespecified as [-asp]. If there is no feature [-asp], the latter solution is not possible. I will account for the lack of aspiration in reduplicated forms using a modified version of the analysis in Mester (1986).

I have argued that the 'diaspirate' roots should in fact be analyzed as roots with a single, root-final aspirated consonant. Under this analysis, as is consistent with the surface facts, Sanskrit does not allow two aspirated consonants in a root. My solution will follow from this fact and from a prohibition on long-distance linking of laryngeal features.

To rule out roots with two aspirates, the language must have two properties: (1) Adjacent [asp] is ruled out by the OCP, and (2) Double linking of aspiration is prohibited, so the OCP cannot be circumvented in this way (McCarthy 1985). Then, I follow Mester's solution to the reduplication problem. He assumes that only aspiration is autosegmentalized; assuming feature geometry all features are autosegmentalized, but this does not affect the analysis. I will therefore describe the modifed analysis that assumes feature geometry. (Mester also assumes diaspirate roots; I will discuss this difference shortly).

112 Laryngeal Features and Laryngeal Neutralization

Mester argues that reduplication involves linking of the melody of a root to another skeleton that initially is not linearized with respect to the skeleton of the root. The two skeleta are later linearized by the independently needed process of Tier Conflation. Because they are separated by a vowel, the original /b^h/ and the reduplicated /b^h/ will have to be given separate Root nodes by Tier Conflation. However, presumably the rest of the features are shared, since the intervening vowel has no features that would block the linking. This means that [asp] is doubly linked, but this is the forbidden configuration; it is repaired by delinking the first consonant from [asp].

(41) (after Mester p. 247)
```
       asp
        \
        b i d
        | | |
        C V C
```

Reduplication
```
       asp   C V
        \ ´ ´
        b i d
        | | |
        C V C
```

Tier Conflation

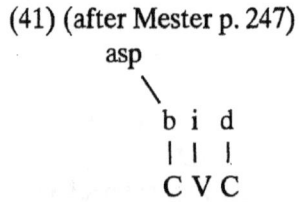

Repair of violation:
```
        asp
        ⤫|
       b i b i d
```

Output : bib^{h}id

Mester (who assumes underlying diaspirate roots) argues that a benefit of his solution is that it need not be restricted by morphological category; the forbidden doubly linked aspiration will only arise because of the way reduplication is done, which will not apply to prefixes. In this revised solution it is necessary to assume that the OCP effect is restricted to underlying forms-- there are no diaspirate roots--but does not hold in the phonology, since there is no OCP effect between aspirates in prefixes and roots. The prohibition on long-distance linking of [asp], on the other hand, is true everywhere. It is true of underlying forms, to rule out diaspirate roots (which could otherwise circumvent the OCP by double linking), and it also applies to the long-distance linking created by reduplication. Restricting the OCP effect to underlying forms is not a problem, since we can certainly refer to roots at that level, and later in the derivation, reduplication is the only process that will result in the forbidden doubly-linked structure. Thus, the solution retains the benefit of Mester's which is that there is no need to refer to the morphological category 'root' later in the derivation, which would be more problematic.

An advantage of this revision of Mester's solution is that underlying diaspirate roots are eliminated. Diaspirate roots would always have one consonant deaspirated by Grassmann's Law, so it is preferable not to represent them as underlying diaspirate if they never surface this way.

Another minor difference has to do with the question of whether the reduplication facts should really be considered as part of the same generalization as GL. As I mentioned earlier, this is a point of some contention. In Mester's solution, all cases are part of the same generalization: Grassman's Law delinks the first consonant from a doubly linked [asp] autosegment in reduplication, and in all the cases of throwback where deaspiration has not already taken place due to another process, such as final deaspiration. In the revised solution, because there are no diaspirate roots, reduplication is the only case where doubly linked aspiration will arise. Thus the delinking of the first aspirate will only apply in reduplication; the other cases end up with a single aspirate due to other rules. So there is a generalization in one sense: you can never have two aspirated root consonants (including copies of root consonants). But there is not a generalization in another sense: the rules that enforce this restriction are not the same in all cases. This solution separates the phenomenon into two separate parts, constraints and rules. The constraints are general to all cases, but the rules are not. Perhaps, then, this is why it has always been so problematic to decide whether GL applies to reduplication or not: previous authors have been trying to give a single answer without realizing that there are two questions. The answer is actually yes AND no: the same constraint is involved in all cases of GL, but the rules enforcing the constraint are not the same in all cases.

The final detail of the solution that must be discussed has to do with ruling out diaspirate roots by forbidding double linking of [asp]. The attentive reader will note that in the analysis of spreading above, there are many cases of doubly linked [asp]; this is needed to account for the facts of consonant clusters. The difference is that double linking is permitted in adjacent consonants (spreading) but long-distance linking is ruled out (GL). There may be a principled reason for this distinction, proposed by Pulleyblank (1989). Pulleyblank discusses the spreading of [nasal] in various languages and what blocks this spreading. He argues that spreading should not be analyzed as blocked by the presence of a feature [-nasal]. Rather, spreading must be local, to immediately adjacent segments; but some segments are not permitted to bear the feature [nasal]. Such segments will block spreading if spreading must be local and cannot 'skip' to the next legitimate bearer of the feature. Double linking of laryngeal features in Sanskrit has the same properties. Laryngeal features spread to adjacent obstruents. But they cannot be doubly linked across vowels: vowels cannot bear the laryngeal features in the phonology, and the linking of consonants across the vowels would not be local. (If this is the correct explanation, it may also help to explain why voice (and other laryngeal feature) assimilation does not cross vowels. However, it remains to explain then why such assimilation can cross sonorants, for instance in Polish.)

3.5.2 Greek

Classical Greek has plain, aspirated and voiced stops. There is assimilation, but it has somewhat different properties from assimilation of voice and aspiration in Sanskrit. Steriade (1982)

Glottalization and Aspiration

gives an analysis of Greek medial and final clusters that relies on double linking of laryngeal features including [-voice]. I will show that this analysis, which is impossible under a theory of privative voicing, is incorrect.

Obstruent clusters agree in laryngeal features. The possible morpheme-internal clusters are given in (42) (Steriade 1982).

(42)
    a. sk sk^h sg sp sb st st^h
    b. kt k^{h}t^h pt p^{h}t^h ps
    c. zd bd
    d. pp tt kk^h tt^h
    e. gm gn dn sm

The first consonant of the obstruent clusters in (42b) may be preceded by a sonorant; for example, /kt/ is possible, so /rk.t, lk.t/ are also possible.

Clusters agree in laryngeal features (Sommerstein 1973). To make this entirely clear a few details must be elucidated. (1) The clusters in (42d) are geminate aspirates, as discussed for Sanskrit. Since these are doubly linked consonants, they obviously share the same laryngeal features. (See Allen 1968). (2) Steriade lists /sb, sg/ as possible clusters. [z] is not phonemic in Greek at this period and so the interpretation of the spelling is a matter of controversy. I will interpret these clusters as actually agreeing in voice (Allen 1968, Sommerstein 1973, Bubeník 1983). (See the discussion of agreement in stop-sonorant clusters below for more discussion). (3) There is also no phonemic aspirated /s/. Thus, /s/-aspirate and /s/-plain clusters both agree in all laryngeal features possible given Structure Preservation.

Steriade's analysis is that spreading only takes place from coronals. But in fact the second consonant of a word-internal stop cluster is always a coronal. Thus the fact that laryngeal features only spread from coronal stops in stop-stop clusters is simply a consequence of the fact that only coronal stops will ever be in the position from which laryngeal features spread; the spreading rule does not have to mention coronals. Rather than specifying that the spreading rule is restricted to coronals, the analysis must state that there is a restriction on stop clusters that the second must always be a coronal. This is not an uncommon requirement; it is true of Latin (Devine and Stephens 1977) and English (discussed in the next section) as well.

If clusters like /sb/ actually did not agree in laryngeal features, the spreading rule would have to say that laryngeal features spread only from stops; if these clusters agreed, as I am assuming, it is the usual rule of spreading of laryngeal features with no further specification.[9]

The facts about clusters in compounds give some additional evidence that this is the correct analysis. Bubeník (1983) gives the following chart of clusters. Clusters with + occur only at morpheme boundary; clusters like /-gd-/ occur only medially, while the others occur initially and medially. Although this is not totally clear from Bubeník's usage, comparison with Steriade's chart shows that in this chart, morpheme boundary actually means compound boundary.

(43)

	pt	bd	$p^h t^h$		
	kt	-gd-	$k^h t^h$		
	k+p	k+b	$k+p^h$		
	k+t	k+d	$k+t^h$	k+s	
	k+k	k/g+g	$k+k^h$		
s+b	sp	zb	sp^h	ps	
s+d	st	zd	st^h		
s+g	sk	-zg-	sk^h	ks	

There are clusters in this list where Spread has NOT taken place despite the fact that the second C is coronal--and these are exactly the cases with a morpheme boundary: /k+t^h, k+d/. Thus the generalization about the level at which laryngeal spread takes place, not Steriade's about what type of Place it spreads from, must be the correct one. Laryngeal spreading takes place only at the level in which stop clusters can only have a coronal as their second member. Thus there is no need to mention [cor] in the spreading rule.

The analysis of these facts, then, is one that is by now familiar. Greek has the Laryngeal Constraint. It has Spreading of laryngeal features, but only below the word level, since compound clusters do not agree in laryngeal features. Clusters across a

Glottalization and Aspiration

compound boundary all have a plain voiceless stop as the first member, since neutralization has already taken place, but there is no spreading. Greek also has a constraint on sequences of stops: the second must be a coronal.

Next consider the facts about word-final consonants and clusters in Greek. The only possible final consonants are /s,n,r/. Final stops delete. There is no evidence for or against the deletion of sonorants other than /n,r/, so I assume that sonorants in general are permitted word-finally. (Since there are no final stops, and no phonemic voice distinction in the fricative, there is no evidence regarding Final Exceptionality.) The possible final clusters are given in (44):

(44)   ls ns ps ks ŋks mps

All of these clusters end in /s/, which is the only permissible word-final obstruent. An obstruent preceding /s/ is voiceless due to the Laryngeal Constraint--laryngeal features will neutralize here, since it is not the licensed position.

Steriade argues that the Greek word template has a special position for word-final /s/. This accounts for the fact that the word-final sequences in (44) do not obey the sonority distance requirement on Greek codas; for example, /ls/ sequences are not possible as word-internal codas although they are possible word-finally. Taking this idea of the specially licensed final /s/ from Steriade, the analysis of the facts about word-final consonants in Greek is as follows. There is a constraint against word-final stops, so that these stops delete. However, if there is /s/ following a stop, it is obviously no longer word-final and so does not delete. The analysis of Greek thus involves the following:

1. Laryngeal Constraint
2. Spreading
3. Sequential constraint: positive constraint
   [-son] [-son]
   [-cont] [-cont]
           [cor]
4. Word-edge constraint:
   *[-cont]#
   [-son]
5. Word-final /s/ is extrametrical (or specially licensed)

The additional final /s/ basically amounts to a coronal appendix, something that is familiar from English. Of course since final stops are prohibited, this appendix can only consist of the coronal fricative.

Steriade (1982) and Ito (1986) give the Greek facts a Coda Constraint analysis. Consider Ito's formalization, which is intended to capture the same generalizations that Steriade makes. The analysis is basically that stops are prohibited in codas, unless doubly linked to a following consonant; geminates and obstruents doubly linked for laryngeal features escape the constraint by the Linking Condition.

(45) Ito's (84)
```
      *C]σ
       |
     [-son]
     [-cont]
       |
     [a asp]
     [b voice]
```

It is crucial to this analysis that there are feature values [-voice] and [-asp], since double linking of these features is what allows many of the clusters to be syllabified. This is impossible under my theory. The objections to this analysis go beyond my desire to argue for privative laryngeal features, however. Steriade needs to make some assumptions that are impossible under current theory, that /s/ is aspirated but that aspiration is not autosegmentalized. This is because she uses the aspiration of /s/ to account for the

Glottalization and Aspiration

cluster facts: the stop-s final clusters are presumed to be syllabifiable because they are linked for [-voice] and [+asp], but the evidence from Grassmann's Law is that /s/ does not behave as if it is aspirated. (The linking for [asp] in final clusters is a purely theory-internal assumption that she can make because there is no contrast in this position; she does not argue that there is any surface evidence of these stops being aspirated.)

In fact, the requirement that the second stop in a cluster be a coronal is crucial, and must be an explicit part of the analysis. For Steriade (and Ito), this is not a separate statement. It is supposed to fall out from the other two parts of the analysis:

1. Coda stops can only syllabify if doubly linked
2. Laryngeal features only spread from coronals

This has the effect that a coda stop will only be doubly linked if the following consonant is coronal, so only those clusters are possible. But this analysis would allow underlying stop clusters that happen to agree in laryngeal features but do not have a coronal in second position. If underlying /gb/ is doubly linked for [voice], it should be allowed, but there are no such clusters. Steriade assumes that clusters that agree in underlying laryngeal features are not linked underlyingly, but this assumption is probably untenable in current theory. One difficulty, for instance, involves how such a grammar could possibly be learned: agreeing clusters are all not linked underlyingly, but all become linked on the surface; how could the underlying representations be discovered? In any case, the analysis would have to somehow prohibit such linked sequences underlyingly, while requiring them later in the derivation; otherwise impossible clusters will be allowed. This attempt to rule out noncoronals in second position by different restrictions on laryngeal features at various levels would be inelegant at best. In fact, the most straightforward way to capture the generalization is for the analysis to explicitly state the sequential constraint about coronals which is true on the surface, and which we see is possible in other languages.

Given that this sequential constraint has been stated, we see that in fact Greek does not have any Coda Condition on stops. The fact that stops delete word-finally may suggest a Coda Condition. But an examination of the word-internal codas shows a rather wider distribution of stops that would be expected if there was some constraint on their appearance. In fact it is incorrect to make a generalization between the word-final facts and the facts about syllable codas in general. The word-final facts are due to a special word-edge constraint; internal codas are not subject to this. Where there obviously is a constraint is in the *second* position in a stop cluster where only a coronal is possible, not in the coda, where any stop can appear.

Another theory-internal point to consider about Steriade's analysis is that all other negative coda constraints described in recent work by Ito are constraints on Place (see Ito 1989). Of course my treatment of laryngeal phonology in this work leans heavily on linking of laryngeal features, but this involves positive licensing rather than a negative constraint. Possibly there are substantive differences between positive and negative constraints despite the fact that they are formally equivalent. More research on positive licensing outside the domain of laryngeal features is needed to determine this.

Finally, it should be mentioned that this revised analysis of Greek does preserve a central result of Steriade's analysis. Steriade notes that unlike other types of deletion in Greek, deletion in stop cluster cases does not lead to compensatory lengthening. The Coda Constraint analysis captures this because the segments that delete are unsyllabifiable; since they have never been syllabified at any level, their deletion will not leave any position open and lengthening will not occur. However, we do not need a Coda Constraint in particular to achieve this, we simply need an analysis that puts restrictions on syllabification, as my analysis also does.

A final detail about Greek has to do with the behavior of stop-sonorant clusters. The possible onsets are:

(46)
    any voiceless stop followed by r,l,n,m
    gr, dr
    bl, gl

Medially, all stop-sonorant clusters involve voiced stops:

(47) gm gn dn bl gl

Glottalization and Aspiration

Steriade also gives evidence that word-initial /gn/ and /dn/ are not tautosyllabic.

Thus, in onsets there are laryngeal distinctions before sonorants at least in some cases: for instance, /pl, p^{h}l, bl/ are all possible onsets. Before nasals, not all distinctions are possible; this is because of the requirement that tautosyllabic clusters be at least four apart on the sonority scale for Greek:

(48)
```
1    2    3  4  5   6
pkt  bdg  s  z  mn  lr
```

Thus, a cluster such as /gm/ cannot syllabify as an onset; word-medially it will always be heterosyllabic. /bl, gl/ can be either hetero- or tautosyllabic; medially the syllabification is optional. It is not clear how the sonority scale can account for this, but it probably has to do with the fact that /l/ and /r/ are not actually of equivalent sonority; for instance, as in English, where final /rl/ is a possible cluster but final /lr/ is not.

This is fairly straightforward, but the odd part is that there are alternations in Greek that involve voicing before sonorants across syllable boundaries. Velars become voiced before /m/-initial inflectional endings and /-mat/, a derivational ending:

(49)
te-teug-mai	'I have happened to'	te-tuk^h-a	'id.'
de-deg-mai	'I have been shown'	dek^h-omai	'to show'
pe-pleg-mai	'I have woven'	plek-o	'to weave'

In these cases, it appears that the stop is already syllabified on the previous cycle. Therefore it is heterosyllabic with the following sonorant, and it becomes voiced--probably because only a voiced stop is possible before a sonorant in a heterosyllabic cluster.

Steriade analyzes this as voicing assimilation that only takes place across syllable boundaries; this is necessary for her analysis, since the stops must be linked to the following sound in order to syllabify in the coda, due to her Coda Constraint. Voicing assimilation from sonorants is impossible if sonorants are underspecified for voicing in the lexical phonology. However, since there are no voiceless velars before a nasal in Greek this could be quite a late rule, happening after sonorants are specified for voicing; this is Steriade's view of these processes. This would not allow us to explain why such sequences never occur in underlying representation, however. There are other rules taking place in the same situation that are clearly not assimilations: for instance, before /m/-initial suffixes, coronal stops become /s/. This suggests that a spreading rule is perhaps not the correct analysis of this case. I will leave the analyses of these cases open, as they have no direct bearing on my main argument. Further discussion of similar facts of English can be found in section 3.6.2 below.

3.6 Apparent counterexamples to the theory

3.6.1 Cambodian

Cambodian is written in a variant of the Devanagari script, and uses the single characters of this alphabet that represent aspirated consonants. Although some descriptive grammars analyze the phoneme system as containing aspirated stops, as implied by the alphabet, linguists (Jenner and Pou 1980, Henderson 1952, Huffman 1972) consider these to be consonant-/h/ clusters. One convincing piece of evidence for this is the fact that these sequences are broken up by infixes, as single consonants would not be:

(50)
    khəŋ 'to be angry'   kɑmhəŋ   'anger'
    khaat 'to lose'   kɑmhaat   'loss'

Thus the stop system of Cambodian consists of plain voiceless stops and the voiced stops /b,d/ which are somewhat implosive. The consonant system is as given in (51) (Huffman 1972):

(51)
    p t c k ʔ
    b d
    m n ñ ŋ
    w   y
      l,r
       s   h

Glottalization and Aspiration

Cambodian does have the Laryngeal Constraint (applying only to [voice], since as there are no aspirated consonants the only laryngeal feature in the language is [voice]). One simple piece of evidence for the Constraint is that syllable-finally, only voiceless stops can appear, never /b,d/. There is additional evidence as well, which requires a closer look at Cambodian syllable structure.

Cambodian words can begin with certain consonant sequences, some of which have a transition sound between the consonants, the nature of which depends on environment. There are three types of initial consonant sequences in Cambodian (summary and chart following Huffman except as noted):

1. No transition sound: C1 is /p t c k/, C2 is /h r s/.

2. Aspiration appears as a transition element between the two consonants: C1 is /p t c k/ and C2 is a sonorant other than /r/, except for the sequence /kŋ/ (This sequence is not noted as exceptional by Henderson).

3. Schwa appears as a transition element between the two consonants: Where C2 is voiced stop or glottal stop; where C1 is a sonorant; in the sequence /kŋ/. (Also in /ss/ clusters according to Henderson. Also according to Henderson, when the first element is a nasal or /l/, no transition sound is also an option.)

(52) Initial consonant sequences
```
        p t c k ? b d m n ñ ŋ w y l r s h
1   p                                 x x x
    t                                 x   x
    c                                 x   x
    k                                 x x x

2   s   x x   x       x x x x x     x x
    p     x x x         x x x       x x
    t   x     x       x x   x x x x
    c   x     x       x x     x x     x
    k   x x x x       x x x     x x x

3   p           x x
    t           x x
    c           x x x
    k           x x x         x
    s           x x x
    ?                             x
    m   x x   x   x   x x         x x x x
    l   x       x x x   x       x x           x
```

Huffman argues that only words with a single consonant onset are what he calls "simple" monosyllables. Words with an initial consonant sequence he calls 'complex' monosyllables; these are distinct from simple monosyllables, and from true disyllables, that have an underlying vowel in the first syllable. He does not give formal representations, but these types can be distinguished as follows. Simple monosyllables and true disyllables contain syllables with a single consonant onset, and a vowel nucleus. 'Complex' monosyllables--those that begin with the sequences in 1-3 above--are phonologically disyllabic, but have no vowel nucleus in the first syllable, as in (53).

(53)

```
              σ   σ
              |   ∧
Type 1    p r a ə    'to use'      [praə]
     2    p k a a    'flower'      [pʰkaa]
     3    p d ə y    'husband'     [pədəy]
```

The representation in (53) is the phonological syllable structure of all initial consonant sequences. The differences among the three classes are differences in surface realization and are determined quite late. Generally, the surface peak of the initial degenerate syllable is voiceless in a voiceless environment and voiced in a voiced environment. In type 2, where aspiration is the voiceless syllable peak (as in, for instance Bella Coola (Hoard 1978)) the first consonant is voiceless. In type 3, where schwa is the syllable peak, the first consonant is a sonorant (which is voiced on the surface, and recall that the syllable peak is determined at a late stage) or the second consonant is voiced.[10]

Infixation gives evidence that the sequences of type 2 are disyllabic and that the transitional aspiration is the syllable peak, not a feature of the initial consonant. The infix is inserted after the first consonant, and no aspiration appears, because the infix has already supplied a nucleus.

(54)
[tʰlɛək]   'to fall'   [tumlɛək]   'fall'
[kʰcɔɔk]   'lame'   [kɔñcɔɔk]   'lameness'

Infixation also shows that type 1 sequences are disyllabic, despite the lack of any syllable peak on the surface. The infix is inserted after the first consonant, and languages are not known to insert infixes into complex onsets (McCarthy and Prince forthcoming):

(55)
traa   'to note'   tɔmraa   'notes'
kliiən   'to hunger for'   kumliiən   'hunger'
[slɔɔ]   'to cook a curry'   [sɔmlɔɔ]   'curry'
[croot]   'to reap'   [cɔmroot]   'harvest'

In type 1 sequences, unlike types 2 and 3, there is no audible syllable peak between the two consonants on the surface. A likely account of this is that these are resyllabified as complex onsets very late in the derivation; most of these sequences are cross-linguistically common possible onsets, unlike types 2 and 3. The only clusters classed as type 1 that are not typical onsets are the stop-/s/ clusters. However, these may actually have the aspirated syllable peak in their surface representation, making them type 2 sequences; aspiration before /s/ would probably be difficult to hear and so these sequences could be misclassified.[11]

It is important that resyllabification of type 1 clusters does not happen until quite late, however. The same as types 2 and 3, type 1 is not a complex onset in the phonology, for two reasons. One is the infixation evidence given above. The other is the fact that there is neutralization in this position: the voiced stops do not appear initially in these sequences. If these sequences were syllabified as complex onsets the Laryngeal Constraint would allow initial sequences like /dr/, which never occur.

Thus the lack of voiced stop-sonorant initial sequences in Cambodian is a result of the Laryngeal Constraint, which also accounts for the lack of syllable-final voiced stops in the language. Although the stop in a stop-sonorant sequence precedes a [+son] segment, they are not in the same syllable, and therefore the stop is not in a position where [voice] is licensed.

The analysis of stop-/h/ sequences as clusters rather than single segments also works for languages related to Cambodian, and in some cases makes sense out of otherwise problematic situations. For instance, Sre is analyzed by Manley (1972) as having a stop system consisting of voiceless, voiceless aspirated, voiced, and implosive. This system does not occur in any other language that I know of. But if there are actually stop-/h/ clusters instead of aspirates (which is the analysis of Smalley 1954), the system is quite normal.

Sre does not allow voiced, implosive, or these 'aspirates' in syllable-final position. Voiced and implosives will be ruled out by the Laryngeal Constraint. If 'aspirates' are clusters, these are ruled out by the fact that there are no stop-initial syllable-final clusters. In this language the presyllables cannot have implosives as their initial consonants, but this does not appear to be an effect of the Laryngeal Constraint in this language, since voiced consonants are possible in this position (the Constraint would neutralize both, since it does so syllable-finally). It is reasonable to consider this a separate constraint since many other segments are ruled out in presyllables: all glides, and all nasals other than /m/.

Syllable-initial clusters make perfect sense if the 'aspirates' are clusters. According to Manley three-consonant initial clusters can only be:

(56)
```
C   l   y
    r   w
```

The first consonant cannot be an 'aspirate'. If aspirates are actually clusters, this is accounted for by the fact that there are no four-consonant clusters, and by the fact that /hl/ and /hr/ sequences are not allowed (they are not possible two-consonant clusters either). Chw and Chy are possible initially; this is accounted for by a slight modification of the above chart, if Ch is a cluster:

(57)
```
C   l   y
    r   w
    h
```

This analysis also makes Sre consistent with related languages that are analyzed as having this consonant system, with Ch clusters, for example Chrau (Thomas 1971).

Another language, Kammu, is described by Svantesson (1983) as having the system voiceless/aspirated/voiced implosive on the surface, but the phonological analysis argues that Ch is a cluster and that the consonant system is actually voiceless/voiced/implosive. In this language there is also evidence from infixes, which can be inserted between C and /h/.

3.6.2 English

English has two voicing phenomena that appear to present a problem for the theory I am presenting. One is the alternation involving voice in the plural and past tense endings; the other is the generalization stated in SPE that obstruent clusters are uniformly voiceless. Mester and Ito (1989) give an analysis of the morphological alternation that is consistent with privative voicing, and I will show that the facts about clusters are more complex than SPE shows. Note that English has only a voicing distinction and so may seem to be out of place in this chapter. I discuss it here because the cluster facts require reference to the similar facts of Greek, discussed above.

  Mester and Ito assume, following the arguments of Pinker and Prince (1988), that the underlying form of the morphemes in question must be voiced, so that for example /z/ is the plural ending.[12] The usual analysis would assume that [-voice] spreads from stem-final consonant to the ending, which is impossible under the privative voicing theory. Mester and Ito argue that instead of a language specific rule of this or any other type, the English alternation should be seen as the result of a universal syllable-wellformedness requirement. If this were a language-particular rule, we would expect to find a language exactly like English except without this rule, which would have examples like *wim[pz]. However, such examples do not occur in any language; they violate the Universal Sonority Generalization described in Chapter 2, which prohibits sequences of syllable peak-voiceless consonant-voiced consonant[13]. Delinking of [voice] from the final consonant repairs this violation, assuming that delinking is the universal default mechanism for restoring well-formedness. The analysis of neutralization presented herein makes exactly that assumption, which Mester and Ito argue is plausible since it introduces no new information and is consistent with Structure Preservation.

  English clusters later than level 1 have no restrictions in voicing; voiced and voiceless obstruents can appear in any order. Tautomorphemic level 1 clusters are much more restricted. SPE says that these clusters must be uniformly voiceless. This generalization would be a problem for a theory of privative voicing, since it cannot state it using [-voice]. The best we could do would be a mirror-image constraint prohibiting [voice] from being linked to an obstruent adjacent to another obstruent:

(58)
$$*\underset{[\text{voice}]}{[-\text{son}]} \quad [-\text{son}] \quad \text{Mirror-image}$$

However, tautomorphemic obstruent clusters are in fact even more restricted than this constraint shows, so this does not seem to be the correct analysis. The correct generalization, as pointed out by Clements (1990) (see also Yip 1991), is that the second consonant must be a voiceless coronal, /t/ or /s/. The exceptions to the voicing constraint amount to only a handful of examples, given in (59), many of which also violate the coronal-second constraint.

(59)
voiced throughout:	husband, rugby, abdomen, wisdom, molybdenum
voiced-voiceless:	lobster, magpie, feldspar, jodphur
voiceless-voiced:	afghan, anecdote, asbestos, sackbut, synecdoche

Names are the only monomorphemic words that are consistently exceptions to these generalizations; many have the phonological properties of compounds. Some of the exceptions listed above appear to be formally compounds as well. *Sackbut* does not combine the morphemes *sack* and *but*, but an English speaker encountering the word for the first time would treat it as a compound, for example by not destressing the second syllable.

The constraints on clusters, then, are similar to the Greek facts discussed above, where the second obstruent in an obstruent cluster must be coronal. As I will show shortly there are other similarities as well.

If the second consonant in the cluster must be /t/, then the only generalization about voicing that must be stated is that the previous consonant must be voiceless. Of course, this can simply be stated, as in (60):

(60)
$$*\begin{array}{cc} [\text{-son}] & [\text{-son}] \\ | & | \\ [\text{voice}] & [\text{cor}] \end{array}$$

This, combined with the restriction that the second obstruent in a obstruent cluster must be coronal, accounts for the facts, and one could simply stop at that.

But the first consonant in the cluster described in (60) would be syllable-final, and the theory already has a mechanism for devoicing syllable-final consonants in the Laryngeal Constraint. English could be a language with the Laryngeal Constraint and Final Exceptionality at level 1 (the latter is needed because English allows word-final voiced obstruents). This analysis is only possible if all word-internal syllable-final consonants at this level are voiceless, so the facts about clusters with sonorants must be considered as well.

Stop-liquid clusters seem to be possible both voiced and voiceless-initial, comparing (61a,b) (the list is not exhaustive).

(61)a. atlas, poplar, antler, butler, cutlery,
    cutlet, fetlock, outlet, platelet
 b. bedlam, hoodlum, maudlin, medlar

Stop-nasal clusters are more interesting. Considering first labial-initial and coronal-initial clusters, there are not many with voiceless obstruents, as predicted. The only exceptions I can find are listed in (62a). This is no more examples than the exceptions to the coronal-second generalization that I began with. However, even the voiceless versions of these clusters are seem to be fairly uncommon, as can be seen from the list in (62b), some of which may not be single morphemes.

(62)
    a. admire, admiral, echidna, kidney, obnoxious
    b. atmosphere, litmus, nutmeg, portmanteau, utmost, nightmare, ointment, chutney, witness, partner, shortening, beatnik, lightning, hypnotize, chipmunk, shrapnel

The situation is reversed, however, when velar-initial stop-nasal clusters are considered. Voiceless-initial clusters are rare (63a), and voiced-initial clusters seem to be the general case (63b).

(63)
    a. acme, acne, drachma, picnic, strychnine, cockney, technical, technique, arachnid
    b. agnostic, magnet, pregnant, signify, pygmy, dogma, quagmire, segment, stigma, stalagmite, augment, enigma, figment, fragment, magma, phlegmatic, pigment, pragmatic, stagnate, significant, signal, prognosis, malignant, magnanimous, magnate, magnify, magnolia, signature, cygnet, assignation, designate, cognate, cognition, diagnose, dignify, igneous, ignite, ignorant

Unsurprisingly in light of the etymology of these words, this is similar to Greek, where all medial velar-nasal clusters must be voiced. The facts for Latin are also similar to those of English. (64) lists the only possible obstruent clusters and stop-nasal clusters in Latin (Devine and Stephens 1977):

(64)   pt kt   ps ks   gm gn

In Latin, stop clusters must have the coronal stop in the second position, and must be voiceless, and the only medial stop-nasal sequences are velar-nasal voiced clusters.

    It seems somewhat unclear whether the facts about English stop-sonorant clusters might be accidental, a result of having inherited so many words from Greek and Latin. If this is the case it might be inappropriate to suggest a phonological analysis. If a phonological analysis is appropriate, in order to maintain the hypothesis that the English cluster facts are a result of the Laryngeal Constraint I must show that these voiced velar-nasal (and stop-liquid) clusters are either voiced later, or not subject to neutralization. Steriade's view of the Greek process is basically the former, that there is postlexical spread of voicing. This analysis is even more problematic in English than in Greek, because there are a few /kn/ clusters, and it should not be possible to have lexical exceptions to postlexical rules. The latter possibility, then, is that voiced velar-nasal sequences are not subject to the Constraint because their initial consonant is not syllable-final. If /gm, gn/ are onsets, then [voice] is in the licensed position and will not delink. /gm/ does not occur word-initially, and although /g/ is occasionally heard in pronunciations of *gnome, gnostic, gnu,* this is hardly conclusive. However, some suggestive evidence that these sequences may be onsets at some level comes from dialects of English that have tensing of [æ] before tautosyllabic voiced consonants. For example, in my (New York City) dialect there is tensing in *bag, cab, sad, ham, can*. There is also tensing in words like *candy, vampire*, as expected; since there are no nasal-stop onsets in English, the tautosyllabicity requirement is met. However, there is no tensing in words like *magnet, fragment* (nor in *abnormal, admiral*, although relevant examples are scarcer). This suggests that velar-nasal clusters may be onsets at some level.[14] The advantage of this analysis over a spreading analysis is that I know of no other cases where the spreading of [voice] is constrained by the place of articulation of the target sound, whereas constraints on syllabification often mention Place. As in the case of Greek, I leave the resolution of this question to future research; if this analysis is untenable, the constraint in (60) is the correct account of the English cluster facts.

3.7 Summary

The following table summarizes the languages discussed. Obviously this chart glosses over some details, which can be found in the text; the concern here is the overall predictions of the theory of neutralization, spread, and Final Exceptionality.

(65)

Constraint	Spread	Final Exc.	Single Feature		Whole node
1.	x			Hupa, Tol	Maidu, Korean, Thai, Klamath,
2.	x	x			Sanskrit, Greek
3.	x	x	x	Bengali	
4.	x		x	Gujarati Marathi	Tojolabal
5.		x			
6.					see below

Possibility 6 is a language with no neutralization or spreading of laryngeal features in consonant clusters. Examples include Georgian (the actual clusters, not the 'harmonic' clusters that can be analyzed as single segments), and Coeur d'Alene (Reichard 1938).

Option 5 is blank because doubly linked [asp] and [gl] structures are rare; the fact that these features spread infrequently is not an argument against this analysis. Recall from the previous chapter that even for [voice], which spreads readily, spreading tends to go hand in hand with neutralization. There are more examples with neutralization and spread of [voice] than with just spread of [voice]. Nonetheless, we must analyze neutralization and spreading as separate operations, because they do sometimes occur separately, and this then gives us the most general explanation of all the cluster phenomena.

Neutralization of all the laryngeal features of a language is more common than neutralization of single laryngeal features. The chart above includes only languages for which I have provided analyses in this chapter. An expanded version of this chart can be found in the appendix to this chapter, including also the languages discussed in chapter 4 and some additional languages that are briefly described. The larger sample there shows more clearly the statistical predominance of neutralization of all features, which constitutes strong evidence that there is a Laryngeal node. The features tend to pattern together more often than not. The presence of the Laryngeal node in the structure of a sound allows us to account for this. It allows us to delete all Laryngeal features with one rule deleting the node, rather than with a separate rule for each feature. If there is a node, a constraint or rule deleting all of the Laryngeal features is simpler than one deleting a particular feature, and so it is not unreasonable to expect that it would be cross-linguistically more common, as is the case.

There is little or no evidence that I have found that argues for more structure under the Laryngeal node. One suggestive point is that single feature constraints on aspiration only are found in languages that have aspiration and voice, but not on voice only. For instance, Bengali neutralizes aspiration and not voice finally, but we find no language identical to Bengali except that it neutralizes voice and not aspiration. I refrain from drawing any conclusions from this for several reasons. One is that the sample of languages with multiple laryngeal distinctions and neutralization is not really large enough to draw any conclusions from this. Note that all of the languages that neutralize aspiration and not voice are related, for instance. Another is that I have found no evidence from other phonological processes (other than neutralization) that any additional structure is needed. Finally, the sort of modification that would be needed to the theory of feature dependency would be rather substantial, and is outside the scope of this work. The problem is that we could explain the fact that we find a language like Bengali but not its opposite by postulating that [asp] is dependent on [voice]. But in the standard model of feature geometry of Clements (1985), a dependent feature can only appear if the feature it depends on is there. This is not true of aspiration, since you can have aspiration without voicing.[15]

Tojolabal is listed under constraints on the whole node in this table. Note that the only laryngeal feature in Tojolabal is [gl]. However, I do not list this as a constraint on a single feature, because there is no reason to state this as a constraint on [gl] in Tojolabal. To eliminate redundancy, the constraint is on the whole node unless more specific information is absolutely required. In the previous chapter, for instance, although those languages have only [voice] as a Laryngeal feature, they should be considered to have the Laryngeal Constraint on the whole node, since that would be their whole Laryngeal node.

3.8 The Binding Hypothesis

In the previous chapter I discussed the predictions of other theories that analyze the facts about consonant clusters as the result of neutralization. These theories all addressed mainly the question of [voice] rather than the other laryngeal distinctions. A theory that addresses laryngeal distinctions in consonant clusters including glottalization and aspiration is that of Kingston (1985,1990), briefly discussed in chapter 1. There I considered the prediction that fricatives pattern with sonorants, since laryngeal distinctions are related to release, and both sonorants and fricatives, unlike stops, have no release. Kingston does not provide a great deal of evidence that this is true in synchronic phonology, and the evidence of phoneme patterning that I discussed showed that fricatives pattern with the obstruents, not with sonorants.

The binding hypothesis of Kingston says that glottal contrasts are bound more strongly to segments that have a release--that is, stops as opposed to fricatives and sonorants. (This idea of release is also used in current work presented by Keating and Steriade). Prevocalic (and possibly also presonorant) stops are released, and I am suggesting that in some languages it is these stops that can bear the laryngeal features. This might suggest that the Laryngeal Constraint could somehow be the result of release. However, it is not possible to account for the neutralization facts by incorporating the notion of release into the phonology, for three reasons:

1. Voicing, unlike the other laryngeal features, is not realized on the release. But all laryngeal distinctions pattern together in neutralization; a theory based on release cannot capture this.

2. As mentioned above, fricatives pattern with obstruents, not sonorants. Imagine that there is a Release node and laryngeal features are dependent upon it. Word-final devoicing cannot be achieved by deleting the Release node, because fricatives (in Kingston's view) do not have Release, and yet they do devoice. The facts of Polish make it particularly clear that with respect to voicing, obstruents form a natural class opposed to sonorants.

3. Even if we confine our attention to obstruents, neutralization and loss of release do not correlate in all cases.

I will now examine these points in more detail.

There are facts that I have discussed that suggest that some aspect of release is important to laryngeal distinctions in clusters. For example, I have discussed geminate aspirates and aspirate clusters in Sanskrit and related languages, where aspiration is realized on the release of the entire cluster although it is phonologically linked to both consonants of the cluster. And there is a similarity between the binding hypothesis and the Laryngeal Constraint: both predict that (at least in some languages) only the last consonant in a cluster is distinctively marked for laryngeal features. But release cannot account for this.

First of all, release would have to be defined in a way that would give fricatives the same type of release as stops but a different type of release from sonorants; yet it would also be necessary to account for the fact that sometimes laryngeal distinctions are neutralized in both sonorants and obstruents (examples of this will be found in chapter 4). Cases where both sonorants and obstruents neutralize laryngeal features could not be analyzed as loss of release. They would have to be quite a different phenomenon theoretically, although there is no empirical basis for this.

But the question of sonorants is somewhat secondary since release does not account correctly for neutralization in obstruents in the first place. The presence or absence of laryngeal distinctions does not always correlate with the presence or absence of release in obstruents. Kingston (1990) discusses the question of languages that do not have neutralization in clusters. It is stated specifically that languages that do not have neutralization are languages where each member of a cluster is released. One example is given, the difference between Yupik and Inupiaq, two Eskimoan languages. Consonants in clusters are released in Yupik, and there is no assimilation; consonants in Inupiaq are "perhaps not" released, and there is assimilation. Presumably this is also how the theory would account for the possibility of laryngeal distinctions word-finally; the prediction is that in all languages with such distinctions, word-final stops are released.

However, if we consider the languages discussed in this chapter it is clear that this correlation does not hold. Data on release was not available for all of these languages, but at least four show neutralization even though consonants in clusters are released: Maidu, Bengali, Tol and Hupa. It is clear that laryngeal neutralization cannot be analyzed as loss of release, since these languages lose laryngeal distinctions without losing release.[16]

Release has a phonetic justification when glottalization and aspiration are considered, since these are realized on the release of the stop closure and sometimes on the release of an entire cluster. But this does not extend to voicing. Languages often have clusters that are voiced throughout, and spectrograms can show voice during the closure period of a stop.

There are some facts about voicing that can perhaps be explained by something about release. This is the fact that voice very commonly spreads in clusters, while spreading of glottalization and aspiration is extremely rare. Since voice can be perceived throughout a consonant cluster, the fact that a cluster is voiced throughout is easily perceived and learned. Since doubly linked aspiration is only realized on the release of the entire cluster in voiceless aspirates, and is partly marked on the release in voiced aspirates, it may be that only more complicated facts about the phonology of the language will reveal this double linking. Thus doubly linked aspiration may more easily be lost from languages historically. However, the binding hypothesis cannot explain this, since it considers all laryngeal distinctions to be dependent upon release, and does not take into account the different behavior of [voice] compared to the other features.

There is obviously some phonetic association between laryngeal features and release. However, the facts accounted for by the Laryngeal Constraint cannot simply be restated in terms of release; the relationship between the phonetics and the phonology is not that transparent. The Laryngeal Constraint may have originally arisen from the phonetic connection between laryngeal articulations and release, but it is now part of the abstract phonological system and cannot be stated in terms of articulatory facts.

The last question that remains is the typology of laryngeal possibilities in consonant clusters. Kingston's theory (1990) states that the following are the possibilities for nonprevocalic stops:

1. Assimilation to prevocalic stop
2. Different from prevocalic stop, but all nonprevocalic stops are the same laryngeally
3. Whole cluster has a constant configuration of glottal articulation: for instance, all prevocalic stops are voiceless and all nonprevocalic stops are aspirated.

(1) is the case of Neutralization and Spread. His example of (2) is Klamath, where nonprevocalic stops are voiceless; this is Neutralization without Spread. (3) is the possibility that is not predicted by my theory, and I will argue that this is correct: this class of languages does not occur, and his analyses of these languages are in error.

Kingston's examples of his type 2 languages are Cambodian and Takelma. He assumes that Cambodian has aspirated consonants, which as I have already shown is incorrect. Section 3.6.1. gives the analysis of Cambodian, and shows that is is a language of his type 2, as it has neutralization only. A crucial point is that this neutralization results in voiceless unaspirated sounds, as in all other cases; there is no rule that aspirates the neutralized stops, as Kingston requires.

Kingston's second example, Takelma, also submits to a similar analysis; again, the assumptions about the phoneme system are the cause of the problem. Kingston uses Sapir's original description of Takelma:

Stop system: Aspirated tenuis
Voiceless media
Fortis (glottalized)
Syllable-final: only aspirated. Glottalized
segments become ?C, instead of glottalized release as elsewhere.
Medial clusters: Prevocalic is voiceless; all
previous are aspirated. (Glottalized consonants do not appear in clusters.)
Initial stop clusters: t^h + voiceless
Final clusters: Only aspirates, except mediae when preceding x,s.

Syllable-final stops, and all preconsonantal stops (with some complications in final clusters), are aspirated. This appears to be a case of neutralization to aspiration, which I predict is impossible--or rather, I predict it would be extremely rare. There is a principled reason that neutralization results in voiceless unaspirated stops: this is the unmarked category, and so will be the result of the delinking. A language where all stops in some position became aspirated would require an additional rule that added the feature [asp]; note that this would require delinking prior to the aspiration rule, if the language has other laryngeal features that are incompatable with aspiration.

The above is true of any neutralization theory. The present theory, in which neutralization is the result of positive licensing conditions, predicts that neutralization to aspiration would be even more complicated. Neutralization happens because laryngeal features are impossible in a particular position. Thus the language would have to have the Constraint at a particular level, where delinking would occur; the Constraint would then have to be inactive later, where the aspiration rule applies, or the aspiration feature would be unlicensed. The evidence is that the Constraint can indeed be active only at a certain level. However, this does make a process of neutralization to other than voiceless unaspirates extremely complex and costly.

It could be true that Takelma is the rare case of this. Its laryngeal phonology is certainly complicated in other respects. The voiced/voiceless distinction is partially but not wholly dependent on stress; glottalized consonants are subject to additional restrictions. However, it seems that it is possible to analyze Takelma neutralization as the usual case of delinking resulting in voiceless unaspirated stops. Shipley (1969) states that Sapir later considered that the consonant system of Takelma might be better analyzed as consisting of voiceless, voiced, and glottalized stops. If this is the case, all non-prevocalic stops are voiceless unaspirated, as predicted:

Stop system: Voiceless
Voiced
Fortis (glottalized)
Syllable-final: only voiceless.
Medial clusters: Prevocalic is voiced; all previous are voiceless
Initial stop clusters: t + voiced
Final clusters: Only voiceless.

Given this analysis and the analysis given of Cambodian above, Kingston's Type 3 does not exist; only Types 1 and 2 occur, as predicted by the theory that neutralization is delinking.

Appendix

This section gathers together all the languages with multiple laryngeal distinctions discussed, in order to show the predominance of neutralization of all distinctions in a language, which is evidence for the existence of a Laryngeal node. Included are the languages analyzed in this chapter and in chapter 4. Also included are a few more languages that I do not analyze in detail, because the data available are somewhat sketchy; these are described briefly below the list. This list certainly does not exhaust the languages that have neutralization, but is intended to be a large enough sample to demonstrate that the asserted difference in commonness of the different types of neutralization is reliable. Note that this does not include languages that have only a single marked laryngeal feature such as Tojolabal and the languages with only [voice] in chapter 2. Given a theory that assumes the existence of a Laryngeal node, such languages have the Laryngeal Constraint stated on the entire node because this is the least redundant formulation of the constraint. However, since there is only one feature involved this does not constitute additional support for the existence of the node.

Whole laryngeal node neutralized: Maidu, Korean, Klamath, Thai, Gbeya, Sui, Iai, Lushai, Kammu, Tolowa, Sanskrit, Greek, Kagate, Ladakhi, Choco

Single feature neutralized: Hupa, Tol, Arbore, Gujarati, Bengali, Marathi

Arbore (Cushitic; Hayward 1984): voiceless, voiced, and glottalized stops, voiced and voiceless fricatives. A rule of word-final devoicing is described, but glottalization does not appear to neutralize: it is not mentioned, and there are examples like

 ša[ɬ c]alɗ 'smallpox'

(The brackets are being used for more narrow transcription of those allophones in this example). The glottalized obstruents in the language are voiced for front articulations, voiceless for back articulations (which is not uncommon; see Greenberg 1970). Unfortunately the grammar does not say whether the devoicing rule applies to the voiced glottalized stops.

Ladakhi (Sino-Tibetan; Koshal 1979): Voiceless, voiced and voiced aspirated stops and affricates; also a murmured lateral, which I would analyze as marked [asp]. Only voiceless obstruents can occur syllable-finally; the murmured lateral also does not appear syllable-finally. There are additional restrictions as well, as no affricates and no palatals appear syllable-finally.

Choco (Loewen 1963): The facts are clearest for the dialect called Waunana (p.329). Stops are voiceless unaspirated, voiceless aspirated, or voiced. Word-finally only voiceless aspirated appear. He also says that in medial clusters before voiceless stops, voiced stops become voiceless and aspirated stops deaspirate. Thus the evidence for neutralization is clear, but unfortunately he does not indicate what happens in clusters before voiced stops, if any. The consonant system of the Sambu dialect has voiceless glottalized, plain voiceless, and voiced stops, and also appears to have neutralization; the only unexplained point is that /g/ can appear word finally. (It may be significant that the only other position where /g/ is possible is intervocalically.)

For details of Gbeya, Sui, Iai, Lushai, Tolowa, Kagate, Kammu, see chapter 4.

Notes

1. The sources disagree in some details of the consonant system but none of the disagreements are crucial. Henderson describes the palatals as affricates and Noss describes them as stops; Henderson lists no /g/ although Noss does; Henderson lists glottal stop and Noss does not. Noss calls the sounds transcribed as /b,d,g/ "unaspirated lenis". However, he describes their allophones in initial position as always being fully voiced, so the facts are the same as those described by Henderson.

   Thai has additional restrictions on syllable-final consonants as well. Aside from the unaspirated stops, the only other sounds that can appear syllable-finally are the nasals. The analysis of this depends on whether the palatals are actually stops or affricates. If they are affricates, the language has a constraint on syllable-final [+cont]. This could be a positive constraint basically like the Laryngeal Constraint (if [+cont], then syllable-initial). If the palatals are stops, there must be an additional constraint against palatals.

2. Kingston decides that glottalized sonorants cannot appear syllable-finally within words, because he cannot find an example of the medial cluster [m'č] from Barker's list, and because there are alternations that show deglottalization. But deglottalization also only occurs in this environment. The examples I give show that Barker's statements about glottalized sonorants in clusters are accurate.

3. There are some examples where the presence or absence of glottalization is unpredictable, which are identified by Barker using a separate morphophoneme ||'||. The examples I am discussing are only those that are phonologically predictable-- these are transcribed by Barker with a glottalized consonant (e.g., m with ' above it in his notation), in contrast with a consonant followed by the morphophoneme '. Since I am not using the latter examples, my transcription uses m' for glottalized consonants.

4. Kim-Reynaud's (1977) summary is helpful in sorting out the terminology of various writers: "Type 1 (p') has generally been characterized as fortis, tense, forced, or glottalized but not

aspirated (called fortis in this study); Type 2 (p) as lenis, lax, weak, and slightly aspirated (lenis); and Type 3 (p^h) as tense and strongly aspirated." p.6 The lenis stops are those that are called lightly aspirated, and the aspirated stops heavily aspirated. The lenis stops are what you get in neutralization, so they are clearly the plain voiceless stops with the stop release being what is interpreted by some writers as 'light' aspiration.

5. Chatterji (1926) discusses voicing assimilation but it is impossible to tell which are synchronic and which diachronic facts; in addition there are disagreements between Chatterji (1921) and (1926), so I am mainly relying on the work of Ferguson. Ferguson (1945) says that Chatterji is wrong in stating that voiced stops devoice before a voiceless stop.

Dimock, Bhattacharji and Chatterjee (1976) also give conflicting data: they say that final aspirated stops are in free variation with unaspirated, and that final voiced velars may devoice. This can simply be interpreted as another dialect, although I suspect that final aspirates are overcareful pronunciations, since the spelling of the word often retains the final aspirate; for instance, Ferguson and Chowdhury (1960) say that there is no contrast of aspiration finally except in very careful speaking styles.

Chatterji (1921) says that the first stop in a stop-stop cluster is "fully exploded", presumably meaning released. The facts about clusters that he gives are unclear, but he does say that an aspirate loses aspiration before another aspirate, so he seems to be aware of the neutralization of aspiration. If he is talking about the same variety of the language, this is evidence that neutralization of laryngeal features cannot be treated as loss of release, since the first consonant in the cluster is released even though it has lost aspiration; this is discussed further at the end of this chapter.

6. It is unclear exactly why they think the second example is relevant, except that they do generally transcribe final [s] as aspirated, just like the stops, and transcribe it as unaspirated here.

Glottalization and Aspiration

7. One example, tɨt/tɨt'ɨm, I assume to be a misprint, since it is included without comment in the group of examples given to illustrate this generalization.

8. Cardona says that medial clusters of more than two consonants are only of the types:

    VC(h)C(h)y   VNC(h)C(h)

If there are aspirated consonants, the optional (h) in those descriptions can be eliminated; the clusters are

    VCCy   VNCC

where C can be any stop including aspirates. However, the clusters he describes, if they include /h/, violate the rule he also describes that deaspirates stops, and the constraint (above) on syllable-final stops. It is hard to know what to make of this since he makes no distinction in his transcription between underlying and surface forms, enclosing all in slant lines. He gives a form /aNkhḍi/ which should become /ankḍi/ by his deaspiration rule.

9. Steriade does note (p215) that all morpheme-internal clusters have a coronal in second position. But since she believes that clusters like /sb/ do not agree in laryngeal features, she does not make this generalization about spreading. Also, although she appears to realize that clusters like [pp^h] are geminate aspirates (p.240), she uses them as additional evidence that clusters with a non-coronal in second position do not agree in laryngeal features. But of course these do agree in laryngeal features if they are geminates.

10. The syllable peak is also schwa when the second consonant is glottal stop. Although neither consonant is voiced in a cluster like /pʔ/ there are other phonetic considerations that probably account for the fact that this sequence does not have aspiration as its transition, since this would mean a very rapid transition from a spread to a constricted glottis. If the surface syllabification is determined late enough to affected by the slight implosion of the voiced stops, then the latter explanation may apply to them as well.

11. Henderson says that clusters with C1 as /s/ (unless C2 is also /s/) have no transition sound, while Huffman classes these as

having aspiration as the transition. Since the difference between these two descriptions is the difference between aspirated and unaspirated /s/ it would also be quite difficult to hear. If they have no transition sounds (class 1) this is unexceptional; like the other cases in class 1, this is cross-linguistically a very common type of consonant cluster. If there is actually aspiration, then they conform to class 2, sequences which cannot resyllabify as onsets and have the voiceless phonetic syllable peak in a voiceless environment. It might also be possible that /s/ itself is the syllable peak.

12. There is a considerable literature on this subject. See for example Harms (1973) and Zwicky (1974).

13. Mester and Ito say that Greenberg's generalization is that syllable-internal obstruent clusters universally agree in voicing. However, he mentions dialects of Karen that have voiceless-voiced initial clusters. I have been unable to obtain more information on these languages, but if it is correct, the less strong generalization as I give it in chapter 2 must be correct.

14. I stole this idea from John McCarthy's marginal comments to a term paper by Roger Schwarzchild. My authority on the form of references does not address the question of how to credit a source of this type.

15. Although the empirical basis for the generalization, as I point out here, is quite weak, having investigated neutralization in many languages I would be surprised if I found a language that neutralized voice and not aspiration. Thus I am somewhat dissatisfied at having no explanation for this generalization. However, I feel strongly that there is not sufficient evidence to attempt an explanation at this point.

If [asp] were dependent upon [voice] one might expect that [gl] was as well. As can be seen from the chart I have less evidence about glottalization than about aspiration. Greenberg (1970) refers to two languages which have a bilabial implosive that devoices word-finally: Iraqw (S. Cushitic) and Basa (Bantu). I have not seen the reference on Basa, but the Iraqw facts appear to be allophonic, not a phonological rule (Tucker and Bryan 1966).

16. Another example of this, combining neutralization and spreading, is Ancient Greek. Kingston (1985) claims that Greek is not a problem for the hypothesis, since the aspiration in the first consonant is not distinctive, but this is inconsistent with his statement about release in the 1990 paper that I am discussing here. Comparing Sanskrit and Ancient Greek, we have two languages that have aspirated clusters. Both have agreement of laryngeal features in clusters, so both my theory and Kingston's consider these languages to have neutralization. In Sanskrit, aspiration is realized on the release of the entire cluster, and it seems highly probable that the first member of such clusters is not released. But in Ancient Greek it seems that both consonants were released and aspirated separately. In my theory this is simply a difference in phonetic realization of the same underlying representation (a geminate aspirate). But for the binding hypothesis this is a serious difficulty. The theory has no explanation of why there is neutralization in Greek, since the released consonants should be able to bear laryngeal distinctions. The theory predicts that release correlates with laryngeal distinctiveness, but actually they can vary independently of one another.

CHAPTER 4

LARYNGEAL PHONOLOGY OF SONORANTS

4.1 Laryngeal features of sonorants

4.1.1 Sonorants and [voice]

Both empirical and theoretical considerations lead to the conclusion that sonorants are not marked with the feature [voice] underlyingly. The theoretical considerations have to do with the theory of underspecification: voicing is predictable in sonorants, and therefore [voice] is redundant and should not be marked. There are also phonological facts that require that sonorants be unspecified for [voice]. A well-known example is Lyman's Law in Japanese (see Ito and Mester 1986). The initial consonant of the second member of a compound becomes voiced by the rule of Rendaku (1a). This rule is blocked if the second word contains a voiced obstruent (1b), but is not blocked by the presence of a sonorant (1c):

(1)
a. maki + suši -> makizuši   'rolled sushi'
   nišiki + koi -> nišikigoi   'brocade carp'
   ko + tanuki -> kodanuki   'baby raccoon'

b. kami + kaze -> kamikaze   'divine wind'
                  *kamigaze

c. ori + kami -> origami   'paper folding'

Of course another type of example that shows that sonorants are unspecified for [voice] is the phenomenon of voicing assimilation discussed in the previous chapters, where [voice] does not spread from sonorants, and in cases such as

Polish we can see that sonorants are actually transparent to the spread of [voice].

Another case that shows that sonorants cannot be marked [voice] in the phonology comes from Burmese (Okell 1969). Burmese has voiced, voiceless, and aspirated stops, and voiced and aspirated sonorants. There is a process of voicing the initial of the second member of a compound, and a noun can be derived from a verb by voicing the initial consonant. Voiceless and voiceless aspirated obstruents can undergo voicing, so for instance /k^h/ becomes /g/, as does /k/. The rule presumably links [voice] to the consonant, and if [asp] is present it deletes, since the two features cannot cooccur in this language. However, the aspirated sonorants do not undergo this rule--there is no change in them in this position. This is evidence that it would be impossible to link [voice] to a sonorant without creating an ill-formed representation. A similar phenomenon is found in Shilluk (Tucker 1955), where voicing of obstruents is involved in marking aspect. Sonorants are unaffected (except that in the active, liquids become voiced stops).

Although sonorants are not marked [voice], they can be marked [gl] or [asp]. Sonorants marked [asp] are generally realized as voiceless or voiceless aspirated, but sometimes murmured. The arguments that voiceless sonorants are marked with the feature [asp] are discussed in the next section. Glottalized and aspirated sonorants are often subject to the Laryngeal Constraint, and the result of neutralization of sonorants is plain *voiced* sonorants. This is additional evidence that these are the laryngeally unmarked segments of this class, since they occur in positions where no laryngeal features are allowed. Also, plain voiced sonorants are never subject to the Laryngeal Constraint, at least in the phonology; this is additional evidence that they are not marked for laryngeal features. Polish, as discussed in chapter 2, has some surface devoicing of sonorants. However, the evidence is that this has to occur at some quite late level, since voicing does not assimilate *from* sonorants to obstruents within words.

Neutralization and sonorants will be discussed in more detail in section 4.2 of this chapter. In section 4.3 of this chapter I will examine some between-word assimilation effects of sonorant voicing, including considering the question of whether sonorants might be subject to the Laryngeal Constraint at a later level after default fill-in of [voice].

4.1.2 Sonorants and aspiration

The existence of voiceless sonorants poses the following problem: I have given evidence that plain voiced sonorants are unmarked for laryngeal features. In the privative voicing theory, obstruents that have no laryngeal features are voiceless. But sonorants have no [voice] feature, yet are voiced on the surface. If a language has voiced sonorants contrasting with voiceless sonorants, then, how can they be distinguished from one another if there is no [-voice]? There are two possible solutions to this problem:

    1. Sonorants are only underspecified for [voice] in languages in which it is a redundant value. In languages that have voiced and voiceless sonorants, [voice] is not redundant in sonorants. In such languages, voiced sonorants are marked [voice], and voiceless sonorants are unmarked. We would expect in such languages to find that sonorants pattern with voiced obstruents in the phonology.

    2. Mester and Ito (1989) propose that "voiceless" sonorants are actually underlyingly aspirated. They give evidence that this is the case for Burmese, and refer to Clements' (1985) arguments that voiceless sonorants in Klamath are underlyingly aspirated.

    I will argue that the second possibility is correct. First I will review the cross-linguistic evidence from consonant systems of languages with voiceless sonorants. Then I will discuss some additional phonological evidence.

4.1.2.1 Patterning of phoneme systems. Maddieson (1984) lists 16 languages that are reported to contain voiceless sonorants. Nine of these languages have aspirated obstruents as well: Yao, Sedang, Lakkia, Sui, Mazahua, Otomi, Chipewyan, and (already mentioned) Klamath and Burmese. Since such languages possess an aspiration distinction, it seems likely that the "voiceless" sonorants are also aspirated. The logic of the argument is that if the language is already using [asp] for the obstruents, it is natural that it should also use this feature for the voiceless sonorants, and it does not complicate the feature system of the language.

Maddieson's source for Aleut (Bergsland 1956) describes the sonorant sounds in question as aspirated. The language also includes aspirated fricatives (although apparently no aspirated stops).

Other cases appear not to have true voiceless sonorant phonemes. In Mongolian (Street 1963) and Irish the sound is an allophone; there are no phonemic voiceless sonorants. In Kaliai, the sound in question is a flapped /r/ described as giving an effect "of aspiration rather than complete stoppage of flow of air;" there is no phonemic distinction.

Thus the majority of these cases are unproblematic; all ten languages discussed up to this point that actually have phonemic voiceless sonorants also have an aspiration distinction in the obstruents. The remaining cases given by Maddieson are Hopi, Gunnuna-Kena and Iai.

Maddieson's table of phonemes for Hopi does not include aspirated obstruents. One of his references (Whorf 1946) says that Hopi has "preaspirated" obstruent phonemes and voiceless sonorants. However, other descriptions of Hopi (Voegelin, Voegelin and Hale 1962, Voegelin 1956, Jeanne 1978) do not include any of these sounds. There is no additional evidence about the dialect of Hopi that Whorf says has these sonorants. One might theorize that what he describes as 'preaspirated' stops is some kind of rare phonetic realization of aspiration, and that therefore the language does have aspiration, accounting for its voiceless sonorants. This seems unlikely, however. Whorf says that the dialects that do not have preaspirated stops have long vowels in the preceding syllable in the corresponding words. This makes it seem more likely that preaspiration is the reflex of a consonant that closes the preceding syllable (perhaps the consonant is underlying a geminate, as in Icelandic). In any case, there is simply not enough evidence known about this dialect to warrant a revision of the theory.

The only information on Gününa-Këna (Gerzenstein 1968) is a 29-page description of its phonemes. The obstruent system is given as voiceless, voiced and glottalized; there are voiced sonorants only except that the laterals are as given in (2):

(2)
    voiceless apico-prepalatal   ɬ
    voiced apico-prepalatal   l
    voiced dorso-prepalatal   ʎ

There is no description of the allophones or of any phonology that would allow one to evaluate whether this is the correct description of the underlying consonant system. (See the discussion of Klamath in chapter 3, for instance, of an example of how a language with aspirated stops can be misanalyzed as having just this consonant system.) More likely, however, is that the voiceless sound is not a sonorant at all, but simply a lateral fricative. (As noted by Maddieson (1984), grammars frequently make this omission in the description of laterals.)

The remaining case is Iai, a language of the Loyalty Islands (Tryon 1968, Haudricourt 1971). Iai has voiced and voiceless stops, and voiced and voiceless sonorants:

(3)

p			t	t̪	č	k
b	bʷ		d	d̪	ǰ	g
ɸ		f	θ	s		x
			ð			
			l̥			
			l			
m̥	m̥ʷ		n̥	ñ̥	ŋ̊	
m	mʷ		n	ñ	ŋ	
w̥						
w			r			

It is rare for languages to have a laryngeal distinction in the sonorants that does not occur in the obstruents (there are no other cases in Maddieson, for instance). Under this analysis, Iai is a case of this--the sonorants have an aspiration distinction while the obstruents do not. There is evidence, however, that this is the correct analysis despite its unusualness.

Tryon is insistent that the voiceless stop phonemes have no aspiration, and it does not seem to be possible to reanalyze the system as a plain/aspirated opposition. However, there are two arguments, phonological and comparative, that it is correct to analyze the voiceless sonorants as aspirated.

The phonological evidence comes from word-final laryngeal neutralization in this language: only a voiceless stop or a voiced sonorant can appear. Note that these are the unmarked cases: a stop with no laryngeal features is voiceless, and a sonorant with no laryngeal features is voiced. If the theory has the feature [-voice] and it appears on voiceless stops and voiceless sonorants, we expect them to pattern together, but this is not the case. Rather the phonological patterning is as predicted by the present theory: the marked cases voiced stops/voiceless (i.e., aspirated) sonorants, as opposed to the unmarked cases voiceless stops/voiced sonorants.

The comparative evidence is that closely related languages do show an aspiration distinction. These languages are described by Haudricourt (1971). He divides the languages into three groups, North, Far North, South, and Loyalty, the latter including Mare, Lifu and Iai. South does not have voiceless sonorants. Far North has voiceless and aspirated stops, and voiced and voiceless aspirated sonorants. North is basically the same. One North language (p 368) has preserved aspiration only in /t^h/ and the sonorants; it might be relevant that this language has fricatives such as /f/ that the other North languages do not. Possibly /p^h/ has become /f/ in this language. In the Loyalty languages, one, Mare, has voiced, voiceless and aspirated stops, and voiceless and voiced sonorants. (He also includes glottalized sonorants; one would like to see additional evidence that these are single segments, since glottalization does not appear to occur elsewhere in the related languages.) This language has the usual unproblematic system, then. The other two, Lifu and Iai, have the same system (voiced/voiceless stops, voiced/voiceless sonorants.) They both have fricatives such as /θ, ð/ which Mare does not have, suggesting that perhaps the aspirates developed into these fricatives.

Haudricourt gives some correspondences between dialects, but not the ones that are useful for the present purpose. He reconstructs the proto-language with voiceless and prenasalized stops only. Aspiration is obviously a later development if his reconstruction is correct, and he only gives reflexes of the original two stop series. Therefore my suggestions about the possible developments involving aspiration are extremely speculative. The important point is that related languages do have aspirated stops, and it does not seem unreasonable to speculate that this distinction once occurred in the stops in Iai, but now is retained only in the sonorants. This would explain how this unusual system developed. It should be kept in mind that whatever the diachronic facts are, the synchronic phonology of Iai is consistent with the hypothesis that the voiceless sonorants are aspirated; it could not be analyzed in a system with the feature [-voice] without loss of generality.

4.1.2.2 Evidence from phonology. As seen in the analysis of Klamath in chapter 3, voiceless sonorants and voiceless obstruents do not pattern together phonologically in Klamath. Additional evidence from the phonology of Klamath that the voiceless sonorants are aspirated comes from the process of lateral assimilation and debuccalization discussed by Clements (1985) (also referred to in this context by Mester and Ito). Mester and Ito also mention that in Burmese voiceless sonorants are sometimes derived from /h/-sonorant clusters. Burmese also has verb pairs that differ in meaning in a regular manner and are distinguished by aspiration of the initial consonant, including both sonorants and obstruents:

(4)

hkwe	'split'	kwe	'be split'
hce?	'cook'	ce?	'be cooked'
hsou?	'tear'	sou?	'be torn'
hnwei	'make warm'	nwei	'be warm'
hlu?	'set free'	lu?	'be set free'
hyo	'slacken'	yo	'be slack'

Unfortunately this does not seem to be a productive synchronic process; there are only about fifty such pairs. Similar facts can be found in Tibetan. Note that the Tibetan sonorants are described as aspirated (not voiceless) by Chang 1968 and Chang and Shefts 1964, and since the languages are related, this supports the analysis of the Burmese sounds as aspirates as well. (Traditional grammars omit these sounds altogether, probably because (as Chang points out) they are not indicated in written Tibetan.)

Tibetan (Chang 1968) also has aspirated/unaspirated verb pairs, which have a causative/noncausative relationship:

(5)
    thuu   'to meet'   tuu   'to cause to meet'
    phar   'to get increased'   par   'to increase'
    chƐƐ   'to get cut'   cƐƐ   'to cause to get
                                                                                                                                                      cut,' i.e., to cut
    ŋhöö   'to get fried'   ŋöö   'to fry'
    ñ hee   'to get tanned'   ñ ee   'to tan'

Chang does not address the question of whether the process is productive, although her analysis of the history implies that it must have been at some point. Tibetan has another relevant process that does appear to be productive: The negative prefix begins with /m/. If it is attached to a verb base with an aspirate initial consonant and high tone, aspiration moves from the verb base initial to the /m/.[1]

(6)
    phaa 'to feel sorry'   mhapaa 'Don't feel sorry'

    Icelandic has a process of sonorant devoicing that also gives evidence that voiceless sonorants are marked with the same feature as aspirated stops. Sonorants devoice before aspirated stops, and the stops are always deaspirated. This can be analyzed as a movement of the aspiration feature from the stop to the preceding sonorant. The rules varies in the dialects as to which sonorants it applies to, but whenever the sonorant devoices, the stop must deaspirate. (Thrainsson 1978a, 1978b). As seen in (7a), [r] devoices in all dialects, and so is never followed by an aspirated stop; in (7b) dialectal variants are given that show the correlation of devoicing and deaspiration.

(7)
   a. [har̥ pa]   'harp'
      [var̥ ta]   'wart'
      [har̥ ka]   'hardness'

   b. [stɛl̥ pa, stɛlpʰa]   'girl'
      [pɔl̥ tI, pɔltʰi]   'ball'
      [kʰam̥par, kʰampʰar] 'whiskers'
      [aim̥ta, aimtʰa]   'mutter'

The next section, on neutralization, includes additional phonological evidence for the correctness of analyzing voiceless sonorants as aspirated: in languages with neutralization, voiceless/aspirated sonorants are neutralized to voiced sonorants. This is to be expected if voiceless sonorants are marked and voiced sonorants are unmarked. This is discussed further at the end of the section.

4.2 Neutralization and sonorants

Turning to the facts of neutralization for sonorants and the Laryngeal Constraint, then, these are the possibilities: If the language has only voiced sonorants, the Constraint will never apply to sonorants, since the language has no sonorants with a Laryngeal node. Thus, the Constraint need not specifically mention that it applies to [-son] segments. The languages in chapter 2, with the constraint on [voice], and most of the languages in chapter 3 are examples.

If the language has laryngeally marked sonorants, there are two possibilities: either the constraint applies to obstruents only, or it applies to both sonorants and obstruents. (I know of no cases in which it applies to sonorants and not obstruents, although there are word-edge negative constraints on marked sonorants only in some languages).

If the constraint applies to obstruents only in languages with laryngeally marked sonorants, it must specifically mention [-son]. Klamath, in chapter 3, is an example. If the constraint applies to obstruents and sonorants, it is of the form in (1) in Chapter 3, not specifying the sonorancy of the licensed segment.

The more general constraint, where both sonorants and obstruents are neutralized, is much more common; I have found only two examples of cases where sonorants are exempt from neutralization. Since the latter case requires a more detailed version of the Laryngeal Constraint, this is not surprising; it means that the simpler grammar is the more common. In the next two sections I will describe languages with laryngeally marked sonorants and neutralization.

4.2.1 Constraint on sonorants and obstruents

In these languages, neutralization applies to both sonorants and obstruents. Thus the Constraint is of the least specific form, as described in Chapter 3: A Laryngeal node is only licensed in the configuration in (8).

(8)

$$\text{Laryngeal node}: \overset{\sigma}{\underset{[+\text{son}]}{\wedge}}$$

This is the same form of the constraint as required for the languages in the previous chapters (with the exception of Klamath). In those languages, the constraint does not apply to sonorants because the language has only plain voiced sonorants, which have no Laryngeal features; the constraint need not specifically apply to sonorancy there, as this would be redundant.

Laryngeal Phonology of Sonorants 159

Gbeya (Samarin 1966) has the following phonemes:

(9)

p	t	k	kp	ʔ
b	d	g	gb	
ɓ	ɗ			
mb	nd	ŋg	ŋmgb	
f	s			h
v	z			
m	n	ɲ	ŋm	
m'	n'			
w	y			
	l			

flaps: v̌   r

Word-internal syllables cannot be closed, but there are word-final consonants. The only consonants that can occur finally are /p t m n ŋ l r y/. Voiced stops and glottalized stops and sonorants are not permitted finally, so this language has the Laryngeal Constraint applying to both sonorants and obstruents as in (8). Prenasalized stops are also not permitted--this may be separate, or it may be evidence that these are marked [voice]. Since doubly articulated segments are also not permitted, it may be that the restriction on prenasalized stops has to do with a prohibition on complex segments, and may be irrelevant to laryngeal features.

Sui (Li 1948) has the following stops and sonorants:

(10)

p	t		k	q
p^h	t^h		k^h	q^h
b	d			
ɓ	ɗ			
m	n	ñ	ŋ	
m^h	n^h	$ñ^h$	$ŋ^h$	
m'	n'	ñ'	ŋ'	

Li describes the glottalized stops and sonorants as preglottalized; I have replaced his transcriptions with standard glottalized symbols. The nasals are described as voiceless; I have transcribed these as aspirated, since as explained in the previous section this is the proper phonological analysis of voiceless sonorants.

Only /m, n, ŋ, p, t, k/ can appear finally, so this language has the Laryngeal Constraint as in (8). Sui also has a number of voiced and voiceless fricatives and voiceless and aspirated affricates, which I have not listed. None of these can appear finally regardless of laryngeal articulation, so this would have to be a separate restriction on final [+cont]. There are plain and glottalized glides, none of which can appear finally, and which will also be accounted for by the [+cont] restriction.

Iai is described in section 4.2.1 above. Its consonant system is unusual in having a laryngeal distinction in the sonorants that it does not have in the obstruents: it has voiced and voiceless stops, and voiced and aspirated sonorants. The voiced stops and aspirated sonorants are the segments that are marked with laryngeal features, and the voiceless stops and voiced sonorants are the unmarked segments. Only the unmarked segments can appear word-finally (there are no word-internal closed syllables), so Iai has the constraint in (8).

Kammu (Svantesson 1983) (Mon-Khmer) is mentioned briefly in chapter 3. The phoneme system as analyzed by Svantesson has voiceless, voiced, and voiced laryngealized stops, and voiced and laryngealized /w/ and /y/. Plain voiced stops never appear on the surface, but are always devoiced; he proposes this system to account for tone differences without having tone in underlying forms. Although this aspect of the analysis is problematic, the existence of laryngealized stops and sonorants seems uncontroversial, and neither can appear syllable-finally. So regardless of the correct interpretation of the rest of the phoneme system it seems clear that Kammu has the Laryngeal Constraint, and it applies to both sonorants and obstruents.

Kagate (Hoelig and Hair 1976) (Tibeto-Burman) has voiceless, voiceless aspirated, and voiced stops, voiced sonorants, and aspirated /r^h, l^h/. Aspirates and voiced stops cannot appear syllable-finally. Lhomi (Vesalainen 1976), a closely related language, has only a voiceless/aspirated distinction in the stops, and has only one aspirated sonorant, /l^h/. Aspirates do not appear syllable-finally.

Lushai (Tibeto-Burman; Henderson 1948, Weidert 1975) has the following consonant system:

Laryngeal Phonology of Sonorants

(11)

p	ph	b	t	th	d	k	kh	?
			tl	tlh				
			ts	tsh				
			tr	trh				
f		v	s		z			h
m	mh		n	nh		ŋ	ŋh	
			l	lh				
			r	rh				

([tr] is described by Henderson as a post-alveolar affricate.) The only consonants that can appear syllable-finally are [p, t, k, m, n, ŋ, l, r]. Thus the Laryngeal Constraint holds of both obstruents and sonorants in this language. There must also be an additional constraint that rules out final [+cont] segments, since fricatives and affricates do not appear syllable-finally.[2]

4.2.2 Constraint on obstruents only

In some languages neutralization applies to laryngeally marked obstruents, but not sonorants. In chapter 3 I give arguments that the Laryngeal Constraint does not apply to sonorants in Klamath. Another language where this appears to be necessary is Tolowa (Smith River Athapaskan) (Bright 1964) which has the following consonant system:

(12)

Unaspirated	b	d		dž		g	g^w	?
Aspirated		t		tš				
Glottalized		t'	ts'	tš'	t̪š'	k'	k$^{w'}$	
Voiceless		ł	s	š	ṣ	x	x^w	h
voiced		l		y		ɣ	w	
voiced	m	n						
glottalized	m'	n'						

Single-segment syllable codas can be only /d, g, ?, s, š, ṣ, h, y, m, n, m', n'/. Aspirated and glottalized obstruents cannot appear syllable-finally, but glottalized nasals can. Thus, the constraint must be restricted to obstruents:

(13)

```
         σ
        ╱ ╲
    [-son] [+son]
      │
   . Laryngeal
```

Glottalized nasals are prohibited syllable-initially. This would have to be a separate syllable-edge restriction; there is no generalization to be made between this restriction and the cases covered by the Laryngeal Constraint. Such separate constituent-edge restrictions often apply to cross-linguistically uncommon laryngeally marked segments, such as glottalized and aspirated sonorants.

The fact that glottal stop is apparently not subject to the constraint is accounted for if glottal stop is [+son], at least in this language. If the glottalized nasals were clusters instead of single segments, the constraint would not have to be restricted to sonorants. However, it would still need to be restricted somehow so that it would not apply to glottal stop, which would then appear syllable-finally singly and in nasal-/ʔ/ clusters, so there is no advantage of simplicity in this analysis. In addition, Bright argues that analyzing glottalized nasals as clusters would complicate the description of clusters in the language: the only possible complex codas are /ʔ, m'/ followed by /s, š, ṣ/.

Although I am arguing that it is possible to restrict the Constraint to [-son], this is not counterevidence to the hypothesis that sonorants are unmarked for [voice]. In those languages with only a voicing distinction, one might try to argue that sonorants are exempt from the constraint because the language has the constraint of the form that applies only to obstruents, as in (13). If the constraint applies only to obstruents, then voiced obstruents will be ruled out syllable-finally, but sonorants could be marked for [voice] and yet still appear syllable-finally.

But the languages in 1.2 show that this analysis is impossible. In these languages the sounds that are permitted syllable-finally are the plain voiceless stops and the plain voiced sonorants. The Constraint cannot be restricted to obstruents in these languages, because glottalized and/or aspirated sonorants are subject to it. So the Constraint does apply to sonorants, but voicing in sonorants is not neutralized. This shows that voiced sonorants are indeed the laryngeally unmarked sonorants.[3]

The evidence from neutralization also confirms the hypothesis that voiceless sonorants are aspirated. If they were marked [-voice], or were unmarked for voice and voiced sonorants were marked [voice], we would expect them to pattern with the voiceless stops. But this is not the case. For example, in Sui, with nasals that are described as voiceless, the possible-syllable-final consonants are the voiceless stops and the voiced sonorants. These pattern together as the unmarked segments, and the voiceless sonorants pattern with the aspirated stops in undergoing neutralization.

4.3 Voice and sonorants at later levels

Polish and Sanskrit, as discussed in chapter 2, have voicing assimilation. In neither language do sonorants participate in word-internal assimilation; in Polish, there is evidence that sonorants are transparent to the spread of [voice]. This can be accounted for by the fact that sonorants are not marked for [voice] in the phonology; if the intervening sonorant has no Laryngeal node, the Laryngeal nodes of the obstruents on either side of it are adjacent. Both languages also have assimilation across word boundaries, which has different properties. In Sanskrit, voice spreads from sonorants across word boundaries. This can be accounted for if sonorants do get a specification for [voice] at this level; this is not unreasonable given that they are voiced phonetically. (Examples from Selkirk 1980.)

(14)
    samyak uktam ->   samyag uktam
    parivaṭ ayam ->   parivaḍ ayam
    tat namas   ->   tad namas

This rule must be different from the word-internal assimilation rule. Voice does not spread from vowels and sonorants in word-internal assimilation. Thus we cannot account for all of the voicing agreement in the language with a single rule. The later rule must involve the word boundaries, as argued by Selkirk (1980).

There is more evidence regarding this difference between word-internal and word-external assimilation in the phonology of Polish. Most analyses of Polish (e.g. Booij and Rubach 1987, Bethin 1989, Gussman ms.) account for both types of assimilation with the same rule: both word-internal and between-word voicing agreement being a result of a postlexical voice spread rule.[4] I will argue that this is incorrect--that voicing agreement at the two levels is achieved at the different levels. This will account for the fact that sonorants behave differently at the two levels.

4.3.1 Polish

First of all, recall that sonorants within Polish words are transparent to voice spread and do not induce voice spread:

(15)
[kr̥ t]an   'larynx'   [grd]yka   'Adam's apple'
mẽ [d]rek   'wiseacre'   mẽ [tr̥ k]owa   'wisecrack (verb)'
[žegwbɨ]   'he would say'
[ńuzwbɨ]   'he would carry'

Across word boundaries, word-final sonorants are transparent to voice assimilation (a); word-initial sonorants block it (b) (examples from Bethin 1989):

(16)
a. [lidr vutki]   'liter of vodka'
   [spazm bulu]   'spasm of pain'
   [žubr dźik'i]   'wild aurochs'

b. [jest mglisto]   'it's foggy'
   [obwok mgwɨ]   'fogbank'
   [odgwos ržeńa]   'sound of neighing'
   [zapax mdloncɨ]   'nauseating smell'

As this data shows, even at this level voice does not spread from sonorants, although the blocking effect seems to imply that they are specified for it. However, in the Krakow dialect (the examples above are from Warsaw), sonorants (including vowels) also induce voice spread across words, similar to Sanskrit:

(17)
brat rodzony	[bradrodzonɨ]	'own brother'
jak nidy	[jagńigdɨ]	'as never'
wóz Andrzeja	[vuzandžeja]	'Andrew's car'

Another process that involves sonorants and voicing is Vowel Raising, which occurs in word-final syllables closed by a voiced obstruent or a [-nasal] sonorant, although there are many exceptions. (Examples from Gussman (1980) although I follow Bethin (1989) and Rubach and Booij (1990) in rejecting Gussman's analysis, which includes a following yer in the environment of the rule).

(18)
Obstruents:
a. Underlying voiced obstruents:

gen.pl.	nom. sg.	
m[ut]	m[o]da	'fashion'
dr[uk]	dr[o]ga	'road'
kr[uf]	kr[o]wa	'cow'

b. voiceless obstruents: no raising
   s[o]k 'juice, nom. sg.'   s[o]ki 'nom.pl'

Liquids: Raising in most native words
a. dw[u]r   dw[o]ry   'court'
   top[u]r   top[o]ry   'axe'
   s[u]l   s[o]li   'salt

b. No raising in borrowed words
   metaf[o]r   metaf[o]ra
   gond[o]l   gond[o]la

Nasals: no raising
   d[o]m   'house'
   k[o]ń   'horse'

Rubach and Booij (1990) and Bethin (1989) account for the different behavior of word-initial and word-final sonorants by differences in syllabification. Some solution like this must be correct; clearly underspecification cannot do the job here, since all of the sonorants should either be specified or unspecified at any particular point in the derivation. But since they are in different syllable positions, a solution could follow from some difference in syllabification. Bethin's analysis has to do with fill-in of [-voice] and so cannot be translated into my framework. R&B's theory is that final sonorants are unsyllabified until very late postlexically. Because they are not incorporated into the prosodic structure, they do not break up the adjacency of the obstruents, and voice can spread. The initial sonorants, however, are adjoined to the word. Assuming that they are fully specified for voice at this point, they will block spreading of voice. I will describe an analysis that roughly follows B&R's ideas about syllabification differences, with one crucial difference: Rubach and Booij say that all voice assimilation, both between and with words, happens at the same time, postlexically. I will show that this cannot work, because of the assimilation facts of the Krakow dialect. I will also consider analyzing these facts by using the Voice Constraint applying at this later level when between-word assimilation applies.

There are two pieces of evidence that word-external spreading is a different rule from word-internal spreading, or at least a rule applying at a different time. One: The difference in external spreading between the Warsaw and the Krakow dialects shows that the external spreading rule must be spreading from obstruents only in the Warsaw dialect. The sonorants must be specified for [voice] by this point in the derivation in the Warsaw dialect in order to block spreading, but they do not trigger spreading. In Krakow on the other hand, all voiced segments induce spreading externally, so the rule is just spread [voice]. But internal spreading is the same in both dialects: [voice] does not spread from sonorants in word-internal clusters:

    okropnɨ   jasni

These words are pronounced the same in Krakow as in Warsaw. Rubach and Booij mention the existence of the Krakow dialect in a footnote, but do not analyze it. It is difficult to see how they would be able to do so. If [voice] spreads from sonorants in Krakow (as we see it does, in (17)), and across-word and within-word assimilation happens at the same time, and if information about structure (like bracketing around words) is gone at that point, then ALL obstruents should be voiced in this dialect except those that are prepausal. This is not only not true in Krakow Polish, but is not true in any known language. Thus their analysis cannot be extended to this dialect. Although this dialect differs only slightly, they would need a quite different analysis, which probably would violate many of the basic assumptions that led them to the analysis for Warsaw Polish in the first place. In fact, it seems that they would need an analysis like the one I am suggesting: The word-external rule must be restricted to apply to certain prosodic structures: to put it simply, it must apply only between words; this must be part of the rule. It is different from the word-internal rule, and so we cannot say that all voicing assimilation in Polish is achieved postlexically. As I will show, my analysis allows us to have only a slight difference in grammars to account for the slight difference in facts in these dialects.

The other piece of evidence has to do with word-initial clusters of the [grdV] type. Consider again the fact that word-internal sonorants are transparent to voicing agreement.

(19)
   a. onsets
      [kr̥ t]an 'larynx'   [grd]yka 'Adam's apple'
   b. word-medial clusters
      mẽ [tr̥ k]owa   'wisecrack (verb)'
      [žegwbɨ]   'he would say'
      [ńuzwbɨ]   'he would carry'

The authors cited above need to derive this fact the same way as they get the facts about word-final sonorants, since they are analyzing word-internal and word-external agreement as the same process. Thus they must say that the medial sonorant is unsyllabified until quite late; they cite as support for this that such segments in examples like those in (b) are commonly deleted in casual speech. But the onsets in (a) are a problem for this analysis, as Rubach and Booij acknowledge in footnote 25. If the sonorant is not syllabified in the onset, then the initial obstruent cannot be syllabified in the onset. But if the first obstruent is not syllabified it should not be able to get voice from the second obstruent, since they claim that voicing assimilation requires prosodic adjacency.

They are attempting to account for all voice agreement in one rule, but they fail, because they need ad hoc statements to account for these onsets.

If voice spread consists of two different rules applying at two different levels, (as argued by Selkirk for Sanskrit) these facts do not present a problem. Word-internal sonorants are transparent to voice spread and do not induce it because they are not specified for [voice] when the rule applies. This makes the correct generalization: both medially and in onsets, clusters agree in voice regardless of an intervening sonorant. Word-external voice assimilation, which behaves quite differently, is a result of a different rule. When word-external voice spread applies, sonorants are specified for voice. This rule treats the word-final and word-initial sonorants differently because of their different syllabification, because the word-external rule must mention prosodic constituency, to account for the fact that is does not apply inside the words. Thus it will be sensitive to the different prosodic structures word-initially and word-finally.

The rule for Warsaw external assimilation is given in (20).

(20)
```
      W    W
     /      \
    σ        σ
     \       |
      ·    [-son]
       ·    |
        · Lar.
           |
        [voice]
```

Unsyllabified (word-final) sonorants, which are not part of the structure, will not block the rule. Word-initial sonorants that are joined to the word result in a different structure as in (21), so that the structural description of the rule is not met and the rule does not apply.

(21)

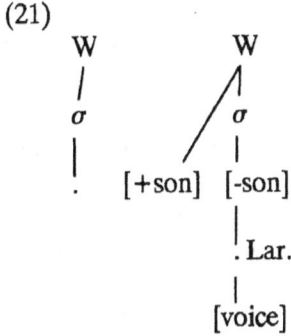

The rule for Krakow, as far as I can determine, would be the same except that the [-son] would be omitted. This predicts that voice only spreads from a word-initial sonorant--that a cluster like [k#tr] would not become [gdr]. None of my sources gives examples of this type, but the descriptions imply that this is correct.

It might also be possible, however, to construct an analysis that relies on the syllabification requirements inherent in the Laryngeal Constraint. Imagine that the Voice Constraint still applies at this late level, restricting the operation of sonorant default voice fill-in. Note that the sonorants that are transparent to voice spread are final sonorants. These are in exactly the position where the constraint would rule out any laryngeal features unless part of a structure linked to a licensed position. However, at this point (after fill-in) they are allowed to BEAR voice. So /r/ in [litr vutki] cannot get voice by default fill in (and note that in [litr] standing alone the [r] would be voiceless on the surface). But, it can get [voice] by spreading from /v/, and of course it will continue to spread to /d/.

On the other hand, the initial sonorants in (16b) are more or less in a position where [voice] is licensed in this language, since they are more or less in an onset. A number of assumptions are necessary, but it could work roughly as follows: The initial sonorant gets default [voice]. It is not exactly in the licensed configuration, since the Constraint does not mention onsets. But if the default [voice] feature fuses with the [voice] of the following consonants, this will be a licensed structure.[5] However, this does not allow us to use the voice feature of the sonorant to block spread, as you might imagine. But recall that the Warsaw Polish spread rule spreads only from [-son]. This rule would not apply because now the initial consonant (from which spreading must happen) is [+son]. In Krakow, of course, where voice spreads from sonorants, there would be spreading from this structure.

Then, perhaps this does allow only one RULE, although it applies at two different times:

Warsaw: Spread voice from [-son], with both rule and Constraint persisting into postlexical phonology, so Constraint applies to sonorant default [voice].

Krakow: Spread [voice]. When the rule applies word-internally, sonorants don't have voice yet, so the word-internal facts are the same as Warsaw. When the rule applies between words, sonorants have gotten default voice where not ruled out by the Constraint, and there will be spreading from them.

The difficulty with this analysis is the same as with B&R's analysis: Why does the rule not "reapply" within words--why doesn't the postlexical spreading rule reach down inside the words and voice ALL obstruents in the language by spreading [voice] from all the vowels and sonorants consonants? This is like cases mentioned by Kaisse (1985:23-4, 1986) and Kenstowicz and Kisseberth (1977:207-8) of apparent Strict Cycle effects in postlexical rules: rules that are demonstrably postlexical, but which do not apply to underived items, or to structures created on an earlier cycle. The Polish case is different in an important way in that these other cases are rules that apply only postlexically. As I have explained above, the Polish rule must apply lexically *and* postlexically, because sonorants behave differently in word-internal and word-external spreading. However, the same issues arise in the case of the Polish postlexical rule if the rule does not mention prosodic structure. If a general solution to this problem of postlexical Strict Cycle effects is found, then it may be possible to maintain this alternative analysis in which the form of the Polish spreading rule is the same both lexically and postlexically. If not, the correct analysis must be the first analysis above, where the external spreading rule is a different rule that explicitly mentions prosodic structure.

The final point to consider is the vowel raising rule. This rule must be lexical, since it has many lexical exceptions. But it must be quite late, for a number of reasons. It is argued by B&R

(1987) that it is a late rule because it follows Yer Deletion, which they say must be postcyclic since it is context-free. We also know that it must be late enough for sonorant voice fill-in to have happened. Also, both B&R and Bethin argue that at earlier levels only sonorants can be codas; so Raising cannot occur until late enough that obstruents can be syllabified in the coda, since that is the environment for the rule.

But although Raising is conditioned by sonorant voicing, underlying obstruent voicing also conditions the rule, although on the surface the obstruents devoice. This looks like a problem: I have argued that word-level neutralization and spread must occur before sonorants are specified for voice. But here we see a rule that is conditioned by the voicing of sonorants, AND by obstruents that later devoice. Thus neutralization is happening after a rule (Raising) that is ordered after sonorant voice fill-in. This seems like a contradiction.

However, this is not a problem because neutralization is the result of a well-formedness requirement, not a delinking rule, so this is not a question of rule ordering at all. [voice] will delink whenever it finds itself in an unlicensed position regardless of when in the derivation this occurs. The [voice] in the obstruent is still present at this late level because before Yer Deletion applies, the obstruent is in an onset, and therefore its [voice] is licensed. When Yer Deletion applies, the obstruent gets resyllabified into the coda. The only tricky part, then, is that Raising must apply while the coda obstruent is voiced, before the delinking caused by its [voice] feature being unlicensed. It is important to note that the obstruent does not lose its [voice] because it is *un*syllabified (contra theories like that of Mascaro and Gussman). It does not lose [voice] until it is actually syllabified impermissibly. This is consistent, because for instance final segments can be voiced underlyingly in languages with the Voice Constraint, since there is no syllabification yet. Thus, the consonant is still marked [voice] when it is syllabified into the coda, at which point the structural description of Raising is met. It could possibly be argued that the fact that Raising applies before the delinking due to the Laryngeal Constraint is due to the Elsewhere Condition, since Raising is the more specific rule.

4.3.2 Meccan Arabic

Additional evidence that sonorants are marked [voice] later in the phonology comes from the postlexical phonology of consonant clusters in Meccan Arabic.[6] There is no spreading:

(22)
    [yafzaʕ]   'fear'
    [ʔakbar]   'older'
    [ʔaǰjar]   'richer'

Postlexically, there is neutralization. The neutralization must be postlexical because it is not structure-preserving, since it creates [p], which is not a phoneme of the language. There is final exceptionality, since voiced word-final consonants are allowed.

(23)
    ʔazfat   [ʔasfat]   'more horrible'
    yizkur   [yiskur]   'he remembers'
    šabka   [šapka]   'engagement'
    ḥabḥab   [ḥapḥab]   'watermelon'

However, there is no neutralization when there are two underlying voiced consonants in a row: the first consonant remains voiced. This is accounted for if there is Fusion.[7]

(24)
    [dabdaba]   'pitter-pat (footsteps)'

There is also no neutralization in a voiced stop-sonorant sequence.

(25)
    [ʔablah]   'more stupid'   *[ʔaplah]

This sequence must be heterosyllabic, from the evidence of other rules of the language. But [b] does not devoice because the sonorant is marked [voice] at this point in the phonology. Thus, Fusion will take place, accounting for the lack of neutralization.

Notes

1. I thank David Odden for pointing this fact out to me.

2. Final [l?, r?] also occur. There is a relationship between presence or absence of glottal stop, vowel length, and tone, and it is not clear that [?] is actually phonemic in this language. Thus the question of these final sequences does not seem to be relevant to the question of phonologically permissible final consonants.

3. It is also possible that the constraint can have additional specifications of other types. For example, Navaho (Sapir and Hoijer 1967) has stops and affricates that are voiceless, aspirated and glottalized; fricatives that are voiced and voiceless; and sonorants that are voiced and glottalized. Glottalized consonants and aspirated stops cannot appear syllable-finally, but both voiced and voiceless fricatives can. This could be analyzed as the Laryngeal Constraint restricted to [-cont]. I suggest this tentatively because I have no other languages of this type and little additional information about relevant phonology of the language.

4. Rubach and Booij also discuss the domain of final devoicing and conclude that it must be the end of the constituent mot, that is, at the end of the prosodic word, not the morphological word as proposed by Bethin (1984). (Note that Bethin (1989) now holds a position closer to the one I am espousing, that voice is only distinctive in onset position.) They choose their formulation on the basis of evidence that they admit is marginal: that when standing alone, the prepositions /w/ and /z/ are not devoiced. But as Bethin points out, this is undoubtedly due to the fact that these must be given a syllable peak to be pronounceable; this means that they are in onset position and will not devoice under any of the formulations of devoicing that any of us hold. She notes that they are in fact pronounced with a schwa, as expected. Prepositions also do not undergo devoicing in sequences like *pod owocem, bez namyslu*. The obvious answer to this is that the final consonants resyllabify and are indeed in onset position; this is Bethin's position. Rubach and Booij say that this is impossible because there is no resyllabification across word boundaries, but since they give no evidence for this assertion and because these facts are

evidence against it, this argument cannot be taken very seriously. Both Bethin and Gussman (ms) assume resyllabification across word boundaries, and Bethin p. 63 discusses a number of other authors who use resyllabification across words boundaries in analyses or descriptions of Polish.

5. A problem with this is that there are cases where the sonorant precedes a voiceless consonant. These appear to be quite rare, however. An examination of Bethin's tables of onsets (p 27-8, reproduced from Sawicka 1974) shows that there are fewer occurring clusters of sonorant-voiceless obstruent than sonorant-voiced obstruent: 5 vs. 13, even if we do not count [f/v] and [š/ž] as obstruents on the grounds that some analyses derive them from sonorants. Bethin (p32) also discusses various statistical studies of text frequency of onset sequences in Polish and sonorant-obstruent onsets are in fact extremely rare. These figures are not given separately for cases with voiced and voiceless obstruents, unfortunately, but given that there are fewer occurring sonorant-voiceless clusters, it seems likely that such clusters occur extremely infrequently.

6. I am indebted to John McCarthy for providing these data from his unpublished field notes.

7. The evidence in chapter 2 suggests that lexically, fusion is a property of languages that have spreading. The facts of Meccan show that postlexically the possibilities may be different.

BIBLIOGRAPHY

Abramson, A.S. 1977. Laryngeal timing in consonant distinctions. *Phonetica* 34: 295-303.

Abramson, A.S. and L. Lisker. 1972. Voice timing in Korean stops. *Proceedings of the International Congress of Phonetic Sciences, Montreal, 1971*, 439-46. The Hague: Mouton.

Agard, F. B. 1950. Structural sketch of Rumanian. *Language* 34 part 2, Language Mongraph 26.

Allen, W.S. 1953. *Phonetics in Ancient India*. Oxford: Oxford University Press.

Allen, W.S. 1968. *Vox Graeca: A guide to the pronunciation of Classical Greek*. Cambridge: Cambridge University Press.

Anderson, S. 1978. Tone features. In Fromkin, V., ed., *Tone: A Linguistic Survey*. New York: Academic Press.

Archangeli, D. 1984. *Underspecification in Yawelmani Phonology and Morphology*. PhD dissertation, Massachusetts Institute of Technology.

Archangeli, D. and D. Pulleyblank. 1986. *The content and structure of phonological representations*. Manuscript, University of Arizona and University of Southern California.

Armstrong, L. 1967. *The phonetic and tonal structure of Kikuyu*. London: Dawsons.

Bargiełowna, M. 1950. Grupy fonemów spółgłoskowych współczesnej polszczyzny kulturalnej. *Biuletyn Polskiego Towarzysta Jezykoznawczego* 22: 25-45. Not seen; referred to by Bethin (ms.)

Barker, M.A.R. 1964. *Klamath grammar*. Berkeley:University of California Press.

Barlow, A. R. 1960. *Studies in Kikuyu grammar and idiom*. Edinburgh: William Blackwood and Sons.

Belchita, A. 1967. Morpheme structure rules in the generative grammar of the Romanian language, I. *Revue roumaine de linguistique* 12: 507-22.

Berendsen, E. 1983. Final devoicing, assimilation, and subject clitics in Dutch. In Bennis, H. and W.U.S. van Lessen Kloeke, *Linguistics in the Netherlands 1983*. Dordrecht: Foris.

Bergsland, K. 1956. Some problems of Aleut phonology. In Halle, M. ed., *For Roman Jakobson*, 38-43. The Hague: Mouton.

Bethin, C. Y. 1984. Voicing assimilation in Polish. *International Journal of Slavic Linguistics and Poetics* 29: 17-32.

Bethin, C. Y. 1989. *Polish syllables*. Manuscript, University of New York at Stony Brook.

Booij, G. and J. Rubach. 1987. Postcyclic versus postlexical rules in Lexical Phonology. *Linguistic Inquiry* 18: 1-44.

Borowsky,T. and R.A. Mester. 1983. Aspiration to roots: remarks on the Sanskrit diaspirates. *Proceedings of CLS* 19: 52-63.

Bright, J.O. 1964. The phonology of Smith River Athapaskan (Tolowa). *IJAL* 30: 101-7.

Browman, C.P. and L. M. Goldstein. 1986. Towards an articulatory phonology. *Phonology Yearbook* 3: 219-52.

Bubeník, V. 1983. *The phonological interpretation of ancient Greek: a pandialectical analysis*. Toronto: University of Toronto Press.

Cardona, G. 1965. *A Gujarati reference grammar*. Philadelphia: University of Pennsylvania.

Catford, J.C. 1977. *Fundamental problems in phonetics*. Indiana University Press.

Chang, B. S. 1968. Voice and aspiration in Lhasa Tibetan. University of California at Berkeley Phonology Laboratory, Monthly Internal Memorandum, August 1968.

Chang, K. and B. Shefts. 1964. *A manual of spoken Tibetan*. Seattle: University of Washington Press.

Chatterji, S. K. 1921. Bengali Phonetics. *BSOAS* 2: 1-25.

Chatterji, S.K. 1926. *Origin and development of the Bengali language*. Calcutta University Press. Reprint 1970, London: Allen and Unwin.

Cho, Y-M. Y. 1990a. *Parameters of Consonantal Assimilation*. PhD dissertation, Stanford University.

Cho, Y-M. Y. 1990b. A typology of voicing assimilation. In *Proceedings of the Ninth West Coast Conference on Formal Linguistics*. Stanford: Stanford Linguistics Association.

Chomsky, N. and M. Halle. 1968. *The sound pattern of English*. New York: Harper and Row.

Clements, G.N. 1987. Toward a substantive theory of feature specification. In *Proceedings of NELS* 18, 79-93. Amherst: GLSA.

Clements, G.N. 1985. The geometry of phonological features. *Phonology Yearbook* 2: 225-52.

Clements, G.N. 1990. The role of the sonority cycle in core syllabification. In Kingston, J. and M. Beckman, *Papers in Laboratory Phonology I*, 283-331. Cambridge: Cambridge University Press.

Clements, G.N. and S.J. Keyser. 1983. *CV Phonology: A generative theory of the the syllable.* Cambridge: MIT Press.

Coats, H.S. and A.P. Harshenin. 1971. On the phonological properties of Russian v. *Slavic and East European Journal* 15: 466-78.

Collinge, N.E. 1985. *The laws of Indo-European*. Amsterdam: John Benjamins.

Davy, J. J. M. and D. Nurse. 1982. Synchronic versions of Dahl's law: the multiple applications of a phonological dissimilation law. *Journal of African Languages and Linguistics* 4: 157-195.

Devine, A.M. and L.D. Stephens. 1977. *Two studies in Latin phonology*. Studia linguistica et Philologica 3. Saratoga CA: Anma Libri.

Dimock, E.C., Bhattacharji, S. and Chaterjee, S. 1976. *Introduction to Bengali*. New Delhi: Manohar.

Dixit, R.P. 1975. *Neuromuscular aspects of laryngeal control with special reference to Hindi*. PhD dissertation, University of Texas at Austin.

Dixit, R.P. 1989. Glottal gestures in Hindi plosives. *Journal of Phonetics* 17: 213-37.

Ferguson, C.A. 1945. *The phonology and morphology of Standard Colloquial Bengali*. PhD dissertation, University of Pennsylvania.

Ferguson, C.A. and M. Chowdhury. 1960. The phonemes of Bengali. *Language* 36: 22-59.

Fleming, I. and R. Dennis. 1977. Tol (Jicaque): Phonology. *IJAL* 43: 121-27.

Flickinger, D.P. 1981. Dissimilation in Gothic without Thurneysen's Law. In Hendrick, R.A. et. al. eds., *Proceedings of CLS* 17.

Furbee-Losee, L. 1976. *The correct language: Tojolabal*. New York: Garland.

Gerzenstein, A. 1968. *Fonología de la lengua Gününa-Këna*. Cuadernos de Linguistica Indigena. Centro de Estudios Linguisticos, University of Buenos Aires.

Giegerich, H.J. 1985. *Metrical Phonology and Phonological Structure*. Cambridge: Cambridge University Press.

Goldsmith, J. 1990. *Autosegmental and Metrical Phonology*. Oxford: Blackwell's.

Goldstein, L. M. and C. P. Browman. 1986. Representation of voicing constrasts using articulatory gestures. *Journal of Phonetics* 14: 339-42.

Gordon, K.H. 1976. *A phonology of Dhangar-Kurux*. Kathmandu: SIL Institute of Nepal and Asian Studies, Tribhuvan University.

Greenberg, J.H. 1970. Some generalizations concerning glottalic consonants, especially implosives. *IJAL* 36: 123-45.

Greenberg, J. H. 1978. Some generalizations concerning initial and final consonant clusters. In *Universals of Human Language v. 2, Phonology*. Stanford: Stanford University Press.

Gussman, E. 1980. *Studies in Abstract Phonology*. Cambridge: MIT Press.

Gussman E. Manuscript. Resyllabification and delinking: the case of Polish voicing.

Halle, M. and K. Stevens. 1971. A note on laryngeal features. *Quarterly progress report, Research Laboratory of Electronics, MIT* 101: 198-212.

Halle, M. and J.-R. Vergnaud. 1980. Three-dimensional phonology. *Journal of Linguistic Research* 1: 83-105.

Harms, R.T. 1973. Some nonrules of English. Reproduced by the Indiana University Linguistics Club.

Haudricourt, A.G. 1971. New Caledonia and Loyalty Islands. In T.S. Sebeok, ed., *Current Trends in Linguistics* v. 8. The Hague: Mouton.

Hayes, B. 1984. The phonetics and phonology of Russian voicing assimilation. In Aronoff, A. and R.T Oehrle, eds. *Language Sound Structure*, 318-328. Cambridge: MIT Press.

Hayes, B. 1986. Inalterability in CV phonology. *Language* 62: 321-51.

Hayward, D. 1984. *The Arbore language*. Hamburg: Helmut Buske Verlag.

Hebert, R. and N. Poppe. 1963. *Kirghiz manual*. Bloomington: Indiana University Press, Uralic and Altaic Series 33.

Henderson, E.J.A. 1949. Prosodies in Siamese. *Asia Major (New Series)* 1: 189-215. Reprinted in Palmer, F.R. Ed., (1970). *Prosodic Analysis*. London: Oxford University Press.

Henderson, E.J.A. 1948. Notes on the syllable structure of Lushai. *BSOAS* 12: 713-25.

Henderson, E.J.A. 1952. The main features of Cambodian pronunciation. *BSOAS* 14: 149-74.

Hirose, H, C.Y. Lee and T. Ushijima. 1974. Laryngeal control in Korean stop production. *Journal of Phonetics* 2: 145-52.

Hoard. J. 1978. Syllabification in Northwest Indian Languages, with remarks on the nature of syllabic stops and affricates. In A. Bell and J.B. Hooper, eds., *Syllables and Segments*, 59-72. Amsterdam: North-Holland.

Hodge, C.T. 1946. Serbo-Croatian phonemes. *Language* 22: 112-20.

Hoelig, M. and Hair, M. 1976. *Kagate Phonemic Summary*. Kathmandu, Nepal: Summer Institute of Linguistics, Tribhuvan University.

Hopper, P.J. 1973. Glottalized and murmured occlusives in Indo-European. *Glossa* 7: 141-66.

Houlihan, K. and G. K. Iverson. 1979. Functionally-constrained phonology. In Dinnsen, D. ed., *Current approaches to phonological theory*. Indiana University Press.

Huffman, F. 1972. The boundary between the monosyllable and the disyllable in Cambodian. *Lingua* 29: 54-66.

Humesky, A. 1980. *Modern Ukranian*. Edmonton: Canadian Institute of Ukranian Studies.

Ingemann, F. and R. Yadav. 1978. Voiced aspirated consonants. In *Papers from the 1977 Mid-America Linguistics Conference*, 337-344. Columbia: University of Missouri.

Ito, J. 1986. *Syllable theory in prosodic phonology*. PhD dissertation, University of Massachusetts at Amherst.

Ito, J. and R.A. Mester. 1986. The phonology of voicing in Japanese: theoretical consequences for morphological accessibility. *Linguistic Inquiry* 17: 49-73.

Iverson, G. 1983. Voice alternations in Lac Simon Algonquian. *Journal of Linguistics* 19: 161-4.

Jeanne, L. M. 1978. *Aspects of Hopi Grammar*. PhD dissertation, Massachusetts Institute of Technology.

Jenner, P.N. and S. Pou. 1980. *A lexicon of Khmer morphology*. Mon-Khmer Studies IX-X, 1980-81. University Press of Hawaii.

Kagaya, R. 1974. A fiberoptic and acoustic study of the Korean stops, affricates and fricatives. *Journal of Phonetics* 2: 161-80.

Kaisse, E. 1985. *Connected Speech: The Interaction of Syntax and Phonology*. New York : Academic Press.

Kaisse, E. 1986. Locating Turkish Devoicing. In *Proceedings of the West Coast Conference on Formal Linguistics 5*. Stanford: Stanford Linguistics Association.

Kálmán, B. 1972. Hungarian historical phonology. In Benkö, L. and S. Imre eds., *The Hungarian language*. The Hague: Mouton.

Katz, D. 1987. *A grammar of the Yiddish language.* London: Duckworth.

Kaye, J. 1979. On the alleged correlation of markedness and rule function. In Dinnsen, D. ed., *Current approaches to phonological theory*, 272-80. Bloomington: Indiana University Press.

Keating, P. 1984. Phonetic and phonological representation of stop consonant voicing. *Language* 60: 286-319.

Keating, P. 1988. A survey of phonological features. Reproduced by the Indiana University Linguistics Club.

Keller, K. 1958. The phonemes of Chontal (Mayan). *IJAL* 25: 44-53.

Kenstowicz, M. and C. Kisseberth. 1977. *Topics in Phonological Theory*. New York: Academic Press

Kim, C.-W. 1965. On the autonomy of the tensity feature in stop classification (with special reference to Korean stops). *Word* 21: 339-59.

Kim, C.-W. 1970. A theory of aspiration. *Phonetica* 21: 107-16.

Bibliography

Kim, Y.-S. 1985. *Aspects of Korean Morphology*. Seoul: Pan Korea Book Corporation.

Kim-Reynaud, Y.-K. 1977. Syllable-boundary phenomena in Korean. Reprinted in Y.-K. Kim-Reynaud 1986, *Studies in Korean linguistics*. Seoul: Hanshin Publishing.

Kimenyi, A. 1979. *Studies in Kinyarwanda and Bantu phonology*. Edmonton: Linguistic Research Inc.

Kingston, J. 1985. *The phonetics and phonology of the timing of oral and glottal events*. PhD Dissertation, University of California at Berkeley.

Kingston, J. 1990. Articulatory binding. In J. Kingston and M. Beckman, eds., *Papers in laboratory phonology I: between the grammar and physics of speech*, 406-434. Cambridge: Cambridge University Press.

Kingston, J. and D. Solnit. 1988. The tones of consonants. Unpublished manuscript.

Koshal, S. 1979. *Ladakhi Grammar*. Delhi: Motilal Banarsidass.

Ladefoged, P. 1971. *Preliminaries to linguistic phonetics*. Chicago: University of Chicago Press.

Ladefoged, P. 1973. The features of the larynx. *Journal of Phonetics* 1: 73-83.

Ladefoged, P. 1979. Review of Catford, *Fundamental Problems in Phonetics*. *Language* 55: 904-7.

Ladefoged, P. 1983. The linguistic use of different phonation types. In Bless, D. H. and J. H. Abbs, eds., *Vocal Fold Physiology: contemporary research and clinical issues*, 351-60. San Diego: College Hill Press.

Ladefoged, P., Williamson, K., Elugbe, B., and Uwalaka, Sister A.A., 1976. The stops of Owerri Igbo. *Studies in African Linguistics*, Supplement 6, 147-63.

Levin, J. 1984. New phonological evidence for laryngeal features. Manuscript, University of Texas, Austin.

Li, F.-K. 1948. The distribution of tones and initials in the Sui language. *Language* 24: 160-67.

Lindau, M. 1982. Phonetic differences in glottalic consonants. *Journal of Phonetics* 12: 147-56.

Lisker, L. 1975. Is it VOT or a first-formant transition detector? *Journal of the Acoustical Society of America* 57: 1547-51.

Lisker, L. and A.S. Abramson. 1964. A cross-language study of voicing in initial stops: acoustical measurements. *Word* 20: 384-422.

Lisker, L. and A.S. Abramson. 1970. The voicing dimension: some experiments in comparative phonetics. *Proceedings of the 6th International Congress of Phonetic Sciences, Prague.* 563-67.

Lisker, L. and A.S. Abramson. 1971. Distinctive features and laryngeal control. *Language* 47: 767-85.

Loewen, J.A. 1963. Choco II: Phonological Problems. *IJAL* 29: 357-71.

Lombardi, L. 1990a. On the representation of the affricate. *UMass Occassional Papers in Linguistics 13*. Amherst: GLSA.

Lombardi, L. 1990b. The nonlinear organization of the affricate. *Natural Language and Linguistic Theory* 8: 375-425.

McArthur, H. and L. 1956. Aguatec (Mayan) phonemes within the stress group. *IJAL* 22: 72-6.

McCarthy, J. 1985. Speech disguise and phonological representation in Amharic. In van der Hulst, H. and N. Smith, eds., *Advances in Non-linear Phonology: Results of the Amsterdam Workshop on Non-linear Phonology, 8-12th August 1983*. Dordrecht: Foris.

McCarthy, J. 1986. OCP effects: gemination and antigemination. *Linguistic Inquiry* 17: 207-63.

McCarthy, J. and A. Prince. Forthcoming. *Prosodic Morphology*.

Maddieson, I. 1984. *Patterns of Sounds*. Cambridge University Press.

Maddieson, I. and J. Gandour. 1977. Vowel length before aspirated consonants. *Indian linguistics* 38: 6-11.

Manley, T. M. 1972. *Outline of Sre structure*. Oceanic Linguistics Special Publication No.12. University of Hawaii Press.

Martin, S.E. 1951. Korean phonemics. *Language* 27: 519-33.

Mascaro, J. 1976. *Catalan Phonology and the phonological cycle*. PhD dissertation, MIT.

Mascaro, J. 1983. *Phonological levels and assimilatory processes*. Manuscript, Universitat Autonoma de Barcelona.

Mascaro, J. Manuscript. A reduction and spreading theory of voicing and other sound effects.

Mayers, M.K. 1960. The phonemes of Pomochi. *Anthropological Linguistics* 2: 1-39.

Mester, R. A. 1986. *Studies in tier structure*. PhD dissertation, University of Massachusetts at Amherst.

Mester, R. A. and J. Ito. 1989. Feature predictability and underspecification: Palatal prosody in Japanese mimetics. *Language* 65, 258-93.

Modi, B. 1986. Rethinking of 'Murmur in Gujarati.' *Indian Linguistics* 47: 165-72.

Mohanon, K.P. 1983. The structure of the melody. Manuscript, MIT and National University of Singapore.

Myers, S.P. 1987. *Tone and the structure of words in Shona*. PhD dissertation, University of Massachusetts at Amherst.

Nacaskul, K. 1978. The syllabic and morphological structure of Cambodian words. In Jenner, P.N. ed., *Mon-Khmer Studies VII*, 183-200. University of Hawaii Press.

Noss, R.B. 1964. *Thai Reference Grammar*. Washington, D.C.: Foreign Service Institute.

Odden, D. 1987. Predicting tone in Kikuria. *Current Approaches to African Linguistics* v. 4. Dordrecht: Foris.

Ohala, M. 1983. *Aspects of Hindi phonology*. Delhi: Motilal Banarsidass.

Okell, J. 1969. *A reference grammar of colloquial Burmese*. London: Oxford University Press.

Pandit, P.B. 1957. Nasalization, aspiration and murmur in Gujarati. *Indian linguistics* 17: 165-72.

Pandit, P.B. 1965. *Phonemic and morphemic frequencies of the Gujarati language*. Deccan College, Poona, Building Centenary and Silver Jubilee Series 34.

Phelps, E. 1975. Sanskrit diaspirates. *Linguistic Inquiry* 6: 447-64.

Pinker, S. and A.S. Prince 1988. On language and connectionism: analysis of a parallel distributed processing model of language acquisition. *Cognition* 28: 73-193.

Pinkerton, S. 1986. Quichean (Mayan) glottalized and nonglottalized stops: a phonetic study with implications for phonological universals. In Ohala, J.J., ed., *Experimental Phonology*. New York: Academic Press.

Pulleyblank, D. 1986. Rule application on a noncyclic stratum. *Linguistic Inquiry* 17: 573-80.

Pulleyblank, D. 1989. Patterns of feature cooccurence: the case of nasality. Arizona Phonology Conference 2, Coyote Papers 9, 98-115.

Reichard, G. 1938. Coeur d'Alene. In F. Boas, ed., *Handbook of American Indian Languages*. Washington: Bureau of American Ethnology, Bulletin 40.

Rubach, J. 1990. Final devoicing and cyclic syllabification in German. *Linguistic Inquiry* 21, 79-94.

Rubach, J. and G. Booij. 1990. Edge of constituent effects in Polish. *Natural Language and Linguistic Theory* 8, 427-63.

Sag, I. A. 1976. Pseudosolutions to the pseudoparadox: Sanskrit diaspirates revisited. *Linguistic Inquiry* 7: 609-37.

Sag, I.A. 1974. The Grassmann's law ordering pseudoparadox. *Linguistic Inquiry* 4: 591-609.

Samarin, W. J. 1966. *The Gbeya language*. Berkeley: University of California Press.

Sapir, E.S. 1938. Glottalized continuants in Navaho, Nootka and Kwakiutl. *Language* 14: 248-74.

Sapir, E. and H. Hoijer. 1967. *Phonology and morphology of the Navaho language.* Berkeley: University of California Publications in Linguistics 50.

Sawicka, I. 1974. Struktura grup spółgłoskowych w jezykach słowiánskich. Wroclaw: Ossolineum. Referred to in Bethin (ms.).

Schein, B. and D. Steriade. 1986. On geminates. *Linguistic Inquiry* 17: 691-744.

Schindler, J. 1976. Diachronic and synchronic remarks on Bartholomae's and Grassmann's law. *Linguistic Inquiry* 7: 622-37.

Selkirk, E.O. 1980. Prosodic domains in phonology: Sanskrit revisited. In M. Aronoff and M.-L. Kean, eds., *Juncture*. Sarotoga, California: Anma Libri.

Selkirk, E.O. 1990a. On the inalterability of geminates. In Bertinetto, P.M. and M. Lopocaro eds., *Certamen Phonologicum II: Proceedings of the Second Cortona Phonology Meeting*. Turin: Rosenberg and Sellier.

Selkirk, E.O. 1990b. A two-root theory of length. *University of Massachusetts Occassional Papers in Linguistics 14*. Amherst: GLSA.

Shipley, W. 1956. The phonemes of Northeastern Maidu. *IJAL* 22: 233-37.

Shipley, W.F. 1963. *Maidu texts and dictionary.* Berkeley: University of California Press.

Shipley, W.F. 1964. *Maidu grammar*. Berekeley: Univerisity of California Press.

Shipley, W.F. 1969. Proto-Takelman. *IJAL* 35, 226-30.

Shukla, S. 1981. *Bhojpuri grammar*. Washington D.C.: Georgetown University Press.

Sigurd, B. 1965. *Phonotactic structures in Swedish*. Lund: Uniskol.

Smalley, W. 1954. Sre phonemes and syllables. *Journal of the American Oriental Society* 74: 217-22.

Sommerstein, A.H. 1973. *The sound pattern of ancient Greek*. Oxford: Basil Blackwell.

Strauss, S.L. 1982. *Lexicalist Phonology of English and German*. Dordrecht: Foris.

Steriade, D. 1982. *Greek prosodies and the nature of syllabification*. PhD dissertation, MIT.

Stevens, K. and D.H. Klatt. 1974. The role of formant transitions in the voice-voiceless distinction for stops. *Journal of the Acoustical Society of America* 55: 653-9.

Street, J. C. 1963. *Khalkha structure*. Indiana University Publications Uralic and Altaic series 24. Bloomington: Indiana University.

Supple, J. and C.M. Douglass. 1949. Tojolabal (Mayan): Phonemes and verb morphology. *IJAL* 15: 168-77.

Svantesson, J.-O. 1983. *Kammu phonology and morphology*. Lund: CWK Gleerup.

Thomas, D. D. 1971. *Chrau grammar*. Oceanic linguistics special publication no. 7. University of Hawaii press.

Thrainsson, H. 1978a. On the phonology of Icelandic preaspiration. *Nordic Journal of Linguistics* 1: 3-54.

Thrainsson, H. 1978b. Dialectal variation in Icelandic as evidence for aspiration theories. In *The Nordic Languages and Modern Linguistics 3*, 533-44. Austin: University of Texas Press.

Trommelen, N. and W. Zonneveld. 1982. *Inleiding in de generatieve fonologie*. Second printing, Muiderberg. Not seen.

Tryon, D.T. 1968. *Iai grammar*. Pacific Linguistics Series B, 8. Canberra: Australian National University.

Tucker, A.N. 1955. *The verb in Shilluk*. Mitteilung des Instituts fur Orientforschung 3, Akademie der Wissenschafter zu Berlin.

Tucker, A.N. and M.A. Bryan. 1966. *Linguistic Analyses: The Non-Bantu Languages of North-eastern Africa*. London: Oxford University Press.

Vago, R. M. 1980. *The sound pattern of Hungarian*. Georgetown University Press.

Van der Hulst, H. 1980. On the formulation of phonological rules. In Daalder, S. and M. Gerritsen, *Linguistics in the Netherlands 1980*. Amsterdam: North-Holland.

Vesalainen, O. and M. 1976. *Lhomi Phonemic Summary*. Summer Institute of Linguistics, Tribhuvan University, Kathmandu, Nepal.

Voegelin, C.F. 1956. Phonemicizing for dialect study with reference to Hopi. *Language* 32: 116-35.

Voegelin, C.F., Voegelin, F.M. and Hale, K. 1962. Typological and comparative grammar of Uto-Aztecan. *IJAL* Supplement 28.1, Memoir 17.

Weidert, A. 1975. *Componential analysis of Lushai phonology*. Amsterdam: John Benjamins.

Weidert, A. and B. Subba. 1985. *Concise Limbu grammar and dictionary*. Amsterdam: Lobster Publications.

Wheeler, M. 1979. *Phonology of Catalan*. Oxford: Basil Blackwell.

Whitney, W. D. 1885. *The roots, verb-forms and primary derivatives of the Sanskrit language*. Reprinted 1945, American Oriental Society, New Haven, Connecticut.

Whitney, W.D. 1889. *Sanskrit grammar*. Reprint 1960, Harvard University Press.

Whorf, B. L. 1946. The Hopi language, Toreva dialect. In Hoijer, H., ed., *Linguistic structures of native America*, 158-83. Viking Fund Publications in Anthropology #6. New York: Wenner-Glen Foundation.

Woodward, M.F. 1964. Hupa phonemics. In Bright, W., ed., *Studies in California Linguistics*, 199-216. University of California Press, Berkeley.

Wurm, S. 1949. The (Kara-)Kirghiz Language. *BSOAS* 3: 97-120.

Yadav, R. 1984. Voicing and aspiration in Maithili: a fiberoptic and acoustic study. *Indian Linguistics* 45: 1-25.

Yip, M. 1991. Coronals, consonant clusters and the coda condition. In Paradis, C. and J.-F. Prunet, eds., *The Special Status of Coronals*. Dordrecht: Foris.

Zilyns'kj, I. 1979. *A phonetic description of the Ukranian language*. Cambridge: Harvard University Press.

Zonneveld, W. 1982. The descriptive power of the Dutch theme-vowel. *Spektator 11*. Not seen.

Zwicky, A.M. 1974. The English inflectional endings. *Ohio State Working Papers in Linguistics* 17, 206-21.

INDEX

Abramson, A.S., 3, 5-10, 15, 21, 93
Aguatec, 23
Aleut, 152
Anderson, S., 20
Andi, 23
Arabic, Meccan, 172
Arbore, 141
Archangeli, D., 34, 71
Aspirates
   constraint on, 78, 80-81, 96-99, 100-2
   as single segments, 81
   voiced, 7-10, 21
   see also Sonorants, voiceless
Basa, 146
Beja, 17
Bella Coola, 125
Bengali, 80-81, 96-97, 133, 134, 137, 141
Bethin, C.Y., 41, 44, 45, 46, 55, 56, 73, 164-66, 171
Binding Hypothesis, 12-15, 134-40
Blocking, 35, 66, 70, 115, 149
Booij, G., 164-67
Borowsky, T., 103-4, 110-11
Browman, C.P., 12
Burmese, 150, 151, 155
Cambodian, 123-26, 138
Catalan, 40-41, 53
Catford, J.C., 8
Chipewyan, 151
Cho, Y.-M. Y., 27, 55, 59-60
Choco, 141-42
Chontal, 23
Clements, G.N., 1, 20, 25, 29, 77-78, 81, 84, 92, 129, 134, 151, 155

Cluster constraints
  English, 12, 127-32
  Greek, 115-23
  Hindi, 10
  Klamath, 85-90
Clusters
  syllable-final
    in Dutch, 33
    in German, 49
    in Polish, 43, 45-46
  and syllable-final delinking, 56-57
  syllable-initial
    in Polish, 41-44, 43-45, 55-57
  vs. single segments, 162. *See also* /h/
Coda Condition, 32, 61-62, 119-22
Coeur d'Alene, 133
[constricted glottis], 3-5
Cooccurrence restrictions
  [asp], 111, 114
  [voice], 25
Dahl's Law (Bantu), 26, 61-70
Delinking as repair, 2, 31-33, 44, 48, 49, 56, 112-13, 128, 171. *See also* Repair
Dixit, R.P., 8, 17
Dutch, 53
  voicing assimilation, 31-34, 36-40
  progressive assimilation, 36-40
Echidna, 131
Elk, A., 148
Elsewhere Condition, 37, 171
English
  clusters, 12, 53, 116, 128-32
  voicing assimilation, 128
Extrametricality, 35, 53-54, 58, 59
Feature geometry
  Laryngeal node, 1, 20, 25, 28, 30, 77, 80, 133-34, 141-42
  within Laryngeal node, 20, 134, 146
Final Exceptionality, 30, 35, 51-52, 53, 58, 72, 73, 81, 100-102, 133
Fusion, 30, 33, 38-40, 109, 172
Gbeya, 142-43, 159

Geminates, 118
  aspirates, 107-9, 115-16, 145
Georgian, 133
German, 39, 49-51, 53, 57
Goldsmith, J., 29, 71
Goldstein, L. M., 12
Gothic, 61, 70
Greek, 107, 115-22, 132, 133, 141, 146
Greenberg, J.H., 18, 19, 23, 30, 141, 146
Gujarati, 81, 100-2
Gununa-Kena, 152-53
Gussmann, E., 41, 44-47, 55, 56, 164-66, 171
/h/
  in clusters vs. aspirated consonants, 81, 101-2, 123, 125-28
  as syllable peak, 124-25
Halle, M., 3-5, 15, 17, 20, 21, 57-58, 70
Harms, R.T., 30, 146
Hausa, 17
Hayes, B., 32
Hindi, 17, 107
Hopi, 152
Hungarian, 52, 53
Hupa, 78, 80, 133, 137, 141
Iai, 141-42, 152-55, 160
Icelandic, 156-57
Igbo, 17
Injectives, 23
Iraqw, 146
Irish, 152
Ito, J., 26-27, 29, 30, 32, 34, 39, 61, 71, 89, 119, 120, 128, 149, 151, 155
Iverson, G.K., 9, 54, 97
Japanese, 26, 149
Kagate, 141-42, 160
Kaisse, E., 170
Kaliai, 152
Kammu, 127, 141-42, 160
Kannada, 53
Kaye, J., 54
Keating, P., 4, 17, 72, 135

Kenstowicz, M., 170
Keyser, S.J., 92
Kikuyu, 61-70
Kingston, J., 12-15, 18, 27, 83, 86, 92, 95, 134-40
Kinyarwanda, 68-69
Kirghiz, 72-73
Klamath
  neutralization/Laryngeal Constraint, 90-93
  phoneme system, 82-85, 151, 155
  sonorants, constraints on, 85-90
Korean
  consonant system, 17, 93-95
  neutralization, 93, 133, 141
  Post-Obstruent Tensing, 95-96
Kuria, 69
Lac Simon Algonquian, 54
Ladakhi, 141-42
Ladefoged, P., 7, 8, 11, 16-18, 93
Lakkia, 151
Laryngeal node. *See* Feature geometry
Levels
  interaction with Constraint, 40-41, 50, 92-93, 128-29, 139, 169, 171
Levin, J., 4
Limbu, 10
Lindau, M., 18, 95
Linking Condition, 32, 35, 37, 119
Lisker, L., 3, 5-10, 15, 21, 93-94
Lombardi, L., 19, 62, 88, 108
Lushai, 141-42, 160-61
McCarthy, J.J., 56, 66, 72, 111, 125
Maddieson, I., 14, 22, 84, 151-53
Maidu, 79-80, 133, 137, 141
Maithili, 9
Marathi, 9
Mascaro, J., 24, 31, 40-41, 48, 55, 171
Mazahua, 151
Mester, R.A., 26-27, 30, 34, 61, 103-4, 110-12, 128, 146, 149, 155
Mohanon, K.P., 24
Mongolian, 152

Index 197

Multiple linking, 31, 32, 64-68, 115, 118
  of [asp] and [gl], 77-78, 111-14, 137
  local vs. long-distance, 114
  See also Geminates
Murmur, 7-10, 21, 101, 110
Myers, S.P., 68, 73
Navaho, 173
Negative constraints, 32, 35, 61, 71, 89, 120
Obligatory Contour Principle, 39-40, 61-70, 111-14
Odden, D., 69
Otomi, 151
Parasitic Licensing, 33, 38
Phonetics
  distinguished from phonology, 2-3, 5, 15-18, 93-95, 99
  of Korean stops, 93-5
  of voiced aspirates, 7-9
  See also Voice Onset Time
Polish, 53, 135
  voicing assimilation
    between words, 164-71
    word-internal, 41-48, 55-56, 59
Pomochi, 23
Prince, A., 56, 72, 125, 128
Prosodic Licensing, 29
Proto-Indo-European
  consonant system, 21-22
Pulleyblank, D., 64, 71, 115
Redundancy Rule Ordering Condition, 34
Release
  and geminate aspirates, 107-9
  and neutralization, 58, 99, 134-40
  vs. phonological aspiration, 91, 99, 100, 144
Repair
  by delinking. *See* Delinking
  by other mechanisms, 48
Resyllabification
  interaction with Constraint, 50, 92-3, 125-26, 171
Romanian, 30, 52, 53
Rubach, J., 50, 55, 164-67
Russian, 21, 28, 60

Sanskrit
   Grassmann's Law, Bartholomae's Law, 103-15
   laryngeal assimilation, 104, 106-7, 109-10
   neutralization, 102-4
   voiced aspirates, 21, 107-11
   voicing assimilation between words, 163, 168
Sapir, E.S., 13, 138-40
scalar features, 11-12
Sedang, 151
Selkirk, E.O., 32, 163, 168
Serbo-Croatian, 30, 52, 53
Shilluk, 150
Sindhi, 17
Siswati, 17
Sonorants
   constraints on, 85-90, 157-61, 162
   devoicing, 21, 43, 45
   laryngeal features, 13-14, 19-20, 77, 82-85, 151-57
   syllabification of, in Polish, 43-46, 55-6, 73, 165-71
   underspecification for [voice], 47, 67, 121-2, 149-50, 163
   voicing assimilation and, 43-46, 71, 121-22, 163-71
   'voiceless' as aspirated, 60, 26, 151-57, 163
Spread
   of [asp], [gl] 77, 102-22, 133, 137
   direction of, 44
   of [voice], 30-35, 6-48, 51, 52, 53, 96-97, 132, 133, 137, 163-64, 166-71. *See also* Dahl's Law
[spread glottis], 3-5
Steriade, D., 11, 24, 32, 92, 114-22, 135
[stiff/slack vocal cords], 3-5
Sui, 141-42, 151, 159-60, 163
Swedish, 48, 51, 53
Syllabification
   interaction with Constraint, 40-41, 50, 92-93, 125-26
Takelma, 138-40
Thai, 25, 81-2
Thurneysen's Law, 61, 70
Tibetan, 155-56
Tojolabal, 100, 133-34
Tol, 78, 80, 97-100, 133, 137, 141

Tolowa, 14, 141-42, 161
Tone features, 21
Tulu, 53
Uduk, 17
Ukranian, 48, 51, 53
Underspecification, 2, 26, 34, 69
   of major class features, 29
   of [voice]. *See* Sonorants
Uniform Applicability Condition, 32
Universal Sonority Constraint, 30, 44, 48, 56, 59, 73, 128
Van der Hulst, H., 31, 36
Verner's Law, 70
Voice Onset Time, 5-12
   and Korean stops, 93-94
Wakashan, 13
Yao, 151
Yiddish, 30, 34-35, 51-52, 53, 72
Yip, M., 129

For Product Safety Concerns and Information please contact our EU
representative GPSR@taylorandfrancis.com
Taylor & Francis Verlag GmbH, Kaufingerstraße 24, 80331 München, Germany

www.ingramcontent.com/pod-product-compliance
Lightning Source LLC
Chambersburg PA
CBHW051059230426
43667CB00013B/2366